What You Might Not Know About
FORGIVENESS

The Seven Key Concepts of Real Forgiveness

BY STEVE DIEHL

D1534010

What You Might Not Know About Forgiveness
By Steve Diehl

Produced for Forgiveness Ministries, Inc.
www.ForgivenessMinistries.com
Info@ForgivenessMinistries.com
(925) 689-6427

ISBN 978-0-9886146-3-5

Printed in the United States of America

CONTENTS

ACKNOWLEDGEMENTS

Writing a book and getting it published is truly a team effort. My name may be on the cover, but without the countless number of people who prayed, encouraged, supported, sacrificed, directed, corrected, etc. over many years this book would never have come to fruition. For this reason I want to first of all acknowledge and thank my wife, Becky for standing by me and encouraging me every step of the way. I would not understand forgiveness the way I do, or be able to communicate it without her participation in the discovery of God's gift of forgiveness. Also my children and extended family, who both helped me learn and practice forgiveness, as well as suffered through my own journey towards healing.

I would also like to thank my church family, the Walnut Creek Friends Church, who always encouraged me (sometimes spurring me on) and gave me the freedom and support to work on this project. The Board of Directors and supporters of Forgiveness Ministries followed in that same kind of support, making it possible for me to have the time to learn and to write.

I would like to mention more than these, but certain people need special recognition: Bob and Janie Washburn, Tom and Maria Coburn, Susan Copeland, Karen Parr, Rita Galusha-Collins, Greg Escher, Linda Kruger, Rich Wallace, Linda John, Melvin Wong and the editors at Armour Publishing in Singapore.

INTRODUCTION

This is a book about forgiveness—*real* forgiveness, the kind of forgiveness that heals the human soul and restores broken relationships. This book is about receiving God's forgiveness, forgiving other people and asking others to forgive us. It is about overcoming self-condemnation and resolving anger towards God. It is about a life-transforming, world-changing forgiveness—a forgiveness that is a gift from God to all of humanity, made possible through Jesus Christ. And it is a book about you.

I don't know the details of your life, but I know some of the most important things about you. I know that God created you so that He and you could enjoy a loving relationship with each other. He created you so that you could enjoy the same things He enjoys. He wants to share His life in all its fullness with you. This is what Jesus was talking about when He said,

> *I came that they might have life, and have it abundantly.*
>
> *John 10:10*

God is not satisfied when people experience anything less than the unimaginable fullness of His life, love and joy.

Again, I don't know the details of your life, but I know that you are not satisfied with how it has gone so far. We all have pains, sorrows and regrets. In fact, you may passionately hate many things that have happened in your life. Life as we experience it now is not how God intended it to be. This is a broken world filled with broken people who

1

do terrible things to one another. You have likely been cheated, abused, abandoned, neglected, mocked, shamed, betrayed, misunderstood and more. Even the most wonderful life on earth has many episodes of sorrow and tragedy. Moreover, if we are honest with ourselves, we would have to admit that we too have done many of these same things to others. We are all wounded and broken people. I may not know the details of your life, but I know that this is true for you because it is true for everyone in this world, including me.

I, myself, passionately hate many things I have done in the past and the things people have done to me. Sometimes I have wished I had never been born. I've wished that I didn't have to see and feel the excruciating pain people inflict upon each other. When I was younger, suicide seemed a reasonable way to escape all this "hell" on earth. However, I learned to survive without losing control. I pretended. I stuffed it deep down inside. I hid from it. I ignored it. I compensated for my failures and the failures of others. I shut down my emotions. I shut people out. I was determined to create my own little world where I could be happy. To some extent, it worked. But was I really happy? Absolutely not! I did all this as a husband, a father, a Christian... even as a pastor.

Tragically, in the church today, there is often great resistance to being real—to being honest with ourselves, with each other and with God. In so doing, we tolerate "hell" in our here and now. To look good on the outside, we hide what is really happening inside. The Bible can even be misused to reinforce this, but this is not what the Bible actually teaches. So in the very place where we should be able to find help, with the very people who should be able to help us, we wear masks. We wear smiles when we feel tears. We go through the motions of worship while feeling angry and resentful. We talk about love while we long for revenge. And we have been led to believe that this is okay.

It isn't.

I became a pastor when I was 28. Having been raised in the church, I was thoroughly indoctrinated in our Western way of thinking about Christianity. In our Western culture, *knowing the right information* is highly valued. Western Christianity tends to follow the same pattern.

It strongly emphasizes our need to believe the right things.[1] Like most Christians, I was convinced that if I simply learned the correct information and believed it, I would experience the fullness of life as God intended. So, I studied the Bible. I even memorized entire books of the Bible. But my personal life still had serious problems. What I didn't know was that I was a broken person. I did have a lot of great information, but that information wasn't fully benefitting me because I wasn't healthy in my soul. Somehow I was missing out on experiencing the life of God, and I didn't know why. I should have known because God had shown me what I needed to focus on in my ministry two weeks before I started as a pastor, but at that time I wasn't ready to fully understand His message.

Two weeks before I began serving as a pastor, God gave me a dream. (I do not say this lightly. I do not claim God-given dreams very often—perhaps only three or four in my life.) I was accustomed to having 'adventure' dreams, dreams that would scare most people, but not me. However, this dream scared me, more than words can explain.

In this dream, I was standing behind the pulpit in my church. It was a Sunday morning and the room was packed. I recognized some faces, but many were strangers. Everyone was well-dressed, polite, happy and attentive. Apparently I was about to preach, but as I inhaled to speak, it was as if two giant hands came from the sides, grabbed the middle of the picture and tore it back, like yanking drapes open. The picture of the people in the pews was pulled aside, and all I could see now was what was behind the picture of the people in the pews—nothing but blackness. It was as if I had gone totally blind. I couldn't see anything. Now you might think that it was the darkness that scared me, but it wasn't. It was the sound I heard in the darkness that terrified me.

I have never heard this sound in real life (though some military people have told me that they have). It was the sound of screaming, wailing, moaning and crying. It was the sound of hundreds of people in excruciating pain, overwhelmed by fear, calling out for help. It was as if a bomb had exploded

---

1   Please don't misunderstand. Knowing truth is absolutely critical. Jesus said, "If you abide in my word then you are truly disciples of mine and you shall know the truth and the truth shall set you free." However, simply having the correct information does not fix everything that needs to be fixed. Learning and believing truth is the solution when we are ignorant or believe lies, but there is more to experiencing life than just having the correct information.

in the room and everyone had been severely wounded, and yet they were still alive in their pain. The sound was horrible beyond imagination. I was terrified.

And then, as quickly as it had been pulled apart, the original picture of a happy, well-dressed congregation came back together. Everyone looked fine, as if nothing had happened.

At this point I was shocked out of my sleep. Instantly wide awake, I lay there beside my peacefully sleeping wife for a long while, afraid to move. I played the images over and over in my mind, listening to the heartbreaking cries of all those people. I didn't know what to do. Then, without expecting an answer, I said to God, "What am I supposed to do with that?" The next thought in my mind surprised me. I heard, "That is what you are going to have to deal with as a pastor, and if you don't, your ministry will amount to nothing."

The next day I shared my dream with Becky and a few others. It didn't take a gifted person to be able to interpret this dream, nor was its meaning anything profoundly new. God was just letting me see *how people can look good on the outside, yet be terribly broken on the inside.* This is true not just for some, but everyone, even me. Unfortunately, it still took many more years and lessons before the message of this dream really changed me. Before that happened, I became increasingly disturbed by three things I had observed about Christians.

1. **The pain of past events can be as intense and powerful today as when they first happened.**

   People have told me of how they had been sexually abused as children or teenagers and are still overwhelmed, even paralyzed by their pain, anger and fear. The same is true for people who have been abandoned, physically abused, verbally abused, etc. It is true not only for people who have been hurt, but also for those who have hurt others. People are burdened with guilt, shame, fear, sorrow and self-condemnation. If it is true that "time heals all wounds," why are they still hurting after all these years? Why is it that so many people are crushed by negative emotions and compulsive behaviors? And why is this true even for Christians? This was especially puzzling when I considered what the Bible says about Christians.

   > *Therefore if anyone is in Christ, he is a new creature; the old things passed away, behold new things have come.*
   >
   > *2 Corinthians 5:17*

What is it about the human soul that can still be intensely affected by events decades old?

2. **People who know the Bible extremely well can still experience tragic failures in their lives.**

    Every year we hear of respected church leaders who fail in their personal lives and ministries. These are people who have seminary degrees, who know the Bible, who are gifted and experienced leaders. A few years ago, a pastor made the front page in our local newspaper because he had been stealing tens of thousands of dollars from his church. Two weeks later he was in the paper because he had committed suicide.

    I know people whom I am convinced are true, born again, Spirit-filled believers, but are alcohol or drug or pornography addicts, or compulsive gamblers, or workaholics, or chronically depressed, or have lost their spouses, etc. How can we explain this?

    Some say that it is the work of Satan, that he is targeting church leaders. I'm sure that Satan does target church leaders—but "greater is He who is in you, than he who is in the world" *(1 John 4:4)*. Jesus is stronger than Satan. Satan alone cannot explain why church leaders with more biblical understanding than most fall to such tragic temptations. Something else is going on, but what?

3. **Learning more truth does not necessarily mean experiencing more of God's abundant life.**

    Even if most Christians didn't fall so drastically, it seemed that somewhere along their walk of faith, many who were committed Christians just stopped growing. They loved Jesus. They were working for Him in many wonderful ways, but their enthusiasm had faded. The discoveries and changes that had energized them became rarer. They used to read new Christian books and go to Christian conferences and get a lot out of them, but not so much anymore. They exuded a "been there, done that" feeling. The Christian life had grown stale and flat.

    Why does Christian growth happen so quickly and easily at the beginning and then flatten out? Are we hitting some invisible ceiling that prevents us from benefitting from Christian activities the way we used to?

These three observations troubled me greatly.

However, God used one more observation, one from my personal life, to drive home my need to focus on the meaning of the dream.

My wife, Becky, is a wonderful woman. However, she is not perfect, nor am I. We are all works in progress[2], which means we still fail to love God and others the way Jesus does. In short, we still sin. When people who sin live together, the sins multiply and pile up.

Typically, at the beginning of a marriage, it's easy to ignore and overlook seemingly little sins, but over time, it becomes increasingly difficult to do so. After 15 years of marriage, with six children in a small house, our sins against each other were reaching a critical point. The most significant symptom was a growing irritation with Becky for little things. She wasn't lazy, beating the children, flirting with other men, abusing drugs or alcohol, etc. No, it was just the little, everyday sins usually born out of fatigue, carelessness, a crowded house and an insensitive husband who wasn't helping her enough.

At first, it was just occasional irritation with Becky. Later it grew to daily irritation. I would suppress my feelings and just try to go on as usual. However, the feelings increased and led to imaginary conversations with Becky. They were imaginary because I didn't want to say what I was thinking and feeling aloud to her. Whenever I had done this in the past, we would end up in an argument for an hour or more, often at midnight, and nothing would be resolved. So the conversations would go on in my head. They would start with statements like:

"How come you never..."

"When are you going to start..."

"I am so tired of when you..."

You can see why these statements always led to arguments when I said them out loud. So I kept them to myself. The problem was that the imaginary conversations became longer and more frequent. At first I could stop them whenever I wanted, but as time went on, I couldn't. They started to take up chunks of time and interfere with other things I needed to think about and do.

---

2   Philippians 2:12—"...work out your salvation, with fear and trembling; for it is God who is at work in you both to will and to work for His good pleasure."

I realized that many of the things I was angry at were real sins, however little they seemed. And if they were sins, I needed to forgive Becky. So I started to work on that. I used everything I knew about forgiveness to try and get rid of my anger towards her and these conversations. I chose to, prayed to, claimed to and pretended to forgive Becky. I acted like I had forgiven Becky. I even believed that I had forgiven Becky. I worked on forgiving Becky for two years, but the anger and the conversations in my head didn't go away!

In fact, after two years of working on forgiving her, the conversations had so dominated my thoughts that I actually measured them to see how bad it was. Sometimes, these imaginary conversations would take up two hours! You might ask, "How could you do that?" Easy, it happened when I was awake in bed at night or in the morning, when I was showering or shaving, when I was doing mindless chores, when I was driving, etc. I would actually have these conversations in my head on Sunday morning as I drove to church to lead worship and preach God's word!

I was trapped in overwhelming emotions and compulsive behaviors, not for any visibly drastic sins, but for lots of everyday ones.

I remember praying one day, "Lord, I am nowhere near divorce, but if I can't get rid of this anger, I don't know where I'm going to be five or ten years from now." I remember saying, "You need to show me how to get rid of anger" rather than just control it (which was what I was doing). I knew this had to be possible because I had memorized a verse where Paul says,

> Be angry, and yet do not sin; do not let the sun go down on
> your anger...
>
> Ephesians 4:26

Here, God is not saying we should simply control our anger (though that is a good thing). Rather, He is saying we must get rid of our anger... in less than a day! Paul knew how to do this. I obviously did not. I knew that it must have something to do with forgiveness, but I didn't know why forgiveness wasn't working for me—a Bible-believing, Bible-memorizing, Bible-teaching, born again, Christ-centered, Jesus-loving Christian! Why couldn't I get rid of my anger, despite working on forgiving Becky for two years?

Then it dawned on me. "Maybe I don't really know what biblical forgiveness is or how to do it."

You see, I was trapped in my anger towards Becky because *I didn't know how to practice authentic, biblical forgiveness. I needed to learn what real forgiveness is, the kind of forgiveness* that God Himself practices, and then follow His pattern. We know this because God tells us in *Ephesians 4:31-32:*

> *Let all bitterness and wrath and anger and clamor and slander be put away from you, along with all malice. Be kind to one another, tender-hearted, forgiving each other, just as God in Christ also has forgiven you.*

As I learned what real forgiveness is and how to practice it as God does, God not only freed me from my anger but also, unexpectedly, showed me the answers to those three troubling observations I mentioned earlier.

I discovered that people continue to be affected by past sins, both their own and those which others committed against them because sins actually damage the human soul, and time cannot heal that damage. Time does not heal; God heals. He heals the human soul when people practice all aspects of His forgiveness. Until we do this, the damage of sin will not be taken away, but will continue to afflict us.

Secondly, when people fail to practice forgiveness well, and thus are not healed by God, they are vulnerable to all kinds of temptations and attacks. Satan attacks us at our points of weakness. Even if Satan isn't attacking us, the fatigue of continually managing the damage of sin can cause a person to give in to temptation more easily. This explains why even Christians with so much Bible knowledge can still experience terrible personal failures.

And finally, when people fail to practice forgiveness well, their Christian growth is hindered and stunted. They grow spiritually to their level of brokenness and then stop growing. Our brokenness is the invisible ceiling through which we cannot penetrate with simply more Bible study and other spiritual disciplines. However, when a Christian practices real forgiveness, and God heals their soul, the ceiling is raised, making more room for growth and transformation into Christ likeness. The believer can experience more of God's life.

I started my forgiveness journey to improve my marriage, but I found that practicing forgiveness is also the foundation for:

- Healing from the damage caused by sins
- Freedom from the emotions of sin (guilt, fear, shame, worry, anger, bitterness, depression, etc.)
- Victory over compulsive behaviors
- Feeling God's love and acceptance
- Joy, peace and fulfillment
- Effective Christian discipleship and growth
- Restoring broken relationships and strengthening good ones
- Stronger families
- Reducing demonic influences and temptations
- Loving our enemies
- Improved physical health
- Effective evangelism and ministry
- And more!

To summarize, practicing forgiveness is how God heals the human soul and creates loving relationships so that we can experience the fullness of His life.

Perhaps you picked up this book because you are struggling with depression, hurt, anger, bitterness, guilt, shame, fear, anxiety or self-condemnation. Or maybe you are struggling with compulsive behaviors, broken relationships or resentment towards God. Or maybe your life has just become flat and boring, and you want more. If that's the case, then I have good news for you. You can experience more, much more. You can experience His abundant life. It will happen as you begin to practice real forgiveness.

If this is something you want, this book is for you. By looking at seven key concepts of biblical forgiveness, we will understand what real forgiveness is and how to practice it. This includes:

- Fully receiving forgiveness from God
- Effectively forgiving others
- Sincerely asking others to forgive you
- Overcoming self-condemnation (often called 'self-forgiveness')
- Resolving anger towards God
- Restoring broken relationships

9

People often ask me why God made forgiveness so difficult. My response is that forgiveness is not very complicated at all. It's actually quite simple and straightforward. In fact, I can teach children forgiveness faster than I can teach most adults. Real forgiveness is not difficult to understand; it's just often **different** from what we've been taught before.

People used to think that the sun revolved around the earth. Everyone was sure that this was true. They couldn't think about the sun and the earth in any other way. Then someone came along and insisted that in fact the earth revolved around the sun. This was very difficult for people to process and accept. They had built their whole understanding of the universe, of life, of the importance of mankind on the premise that we humans were the center of the universe.

Anytime we humans are faced with a new way of thinking, even if it is true, we feel caught off guard, confused, threatened, fearful and defensive. We always tend to think that what we've always believed must be true.

I'm sure that some, perhaps most, of what you know about forgiveness is true. However, there may be some truths about real forgiveness that you might not know. This was certainly true for me. That's why, after spending two years trying to forgive Becky and failing to do so, I asked God to teach me. I started over. I assumed nothing. I discovered that there were many things about forgiveness I didn't know. I have written this book to help you discover what you might not know about real forgiveness.

When I realized that I wasn't practicing forgiveness well, I prayed,

> *Lord, perhaps my understanding of forgiveness is incomplete or even incorrect, since I cannot seem to do it. I need you to teach me. What is real forgiveness and how can I do it so I can become free of this anger? Please teach me.*

That was the turning point for me. I needed to humble myself and admit that I didn't know as much about real forgiveness as I thought I did. I needed to ask God for help.

If you haven't already done this, I want to invite you to ask God to be your Teacher, too. This book is not your teacher. It just contains information gathered and assembled from the Bible which God can use to help you unwrap His wonderful gift of forgiveness. Just reading this book and hearing the right information will not be enough. You need to let God be your teacher. So, I encourage you to stop for a moment right now and pray. Ask God to teach you, to show you, what His gift of forgiveness really is and how to practice it just as He does. He wants to answer that prayer.

Then you can jump right in and we'll look at the first key that unlocks the treasure of real forgiveness.

CHAPTER ONE

Why Your Life Is Not the Way You Want It to Be

The First Key Concept of Forgiveness

Sin damages the human soul
and destroys loving relationships.

Forgiveness is God's solution to a problem He calls sin. To understand the nature of a solution, we must first understand the nature of the problem.

Sin is a big problem—*the* problem for humans. God describes sin in many ways: sin is evil, sin is rejection of God, sin is lawlessness, sin is 'falling short'. God also informs us that sin the opposite of *love*.

When Jesus was asked,

> *"Teacher, which is the great commandment in the Law?"*
>
> *And He said to him, "'You shall love the LORD your God with all your heart, and with all your soul, and with all your mind.' This is the great and foremost commandment. The second is like it, 'You shall love your neighbor as yourself.' On these two commandments depend the whole Law and the Prophets."*

Matthew 22:36-40

It is important to note that not only the first two and greatest commandments from God are about love, but also "the whole Law and the Prophets" are based on love. This means that God's every command is about loving Him and loving others.

Paul said it this way,

> *Owe nothing to anyone except to love one another; for he who loves his neighbor has fulfilled the law. For this, "You shall not commit adultery, you shall not murder, you shall not steal, you shall not covet," and if there is any other commandment, it is summed up in this saying, "You shall love your neighbor as yourself." Love does no wrong to a neighbor; therefore love is the fulfillment of the law.*

Romans 13:8-10

Evidently, love and sin are opposites. When a person is loving God, he isn't sinning. When a person is sinning, he isn't loving God—which includes loving others. Love is what God created us for. However, we don't naturally love God or others. We tend to love ourselves over anyone or anything else because there is something about loving God and loving others that we don't like.

13

What Is Love?

Here is a statement that summarizes and captures much of what the Bible says about love:

> *Love is the self-determined and unhinderable willingness to sacrifice self for the well-being of others.*

Let's look at this statement a little closer.

Real love is *self-determined*. This means that the lover loves not because of something in the one being loved, but something in themselves. God loves us not because there is something in us that causes Him to love us.

People find this reality almost impossible to grasp because it is so different from the 'love' we have grown up with. In this sinful world, what people often call love is not really love. In this world, people love us conditionally —*if, when, because and as long as.*

> **Love is the self-determined and unhinderable willingness to sacrifice self for the well-being of others.**

People love us *if* we are good enough, *if* we are strong enough, *if* we are pretty enough.

People love us *when* we do well, *when* we make them look good, *when* we do what they want us to.

People love us because they like what we have, *because* we cooperate, *because* we like what they like.

People love us *as long as we* make them feel good, *as long as* we do what they say, as long as we fit into their plans, etc.

The world's love is *conditional*, but real love, God's love, is *unconditional*. God does not say, "I love you when..." or "I love you as long as..." God just says, "I love you!" The world 'loves' us because of something in us. God loves us because of something *in Him*. As the Bible says, "God is love" *(1 John 4:7-8)*. Because His love is self-determined and results from His own character, God's love for us—for you—is unconditional and therefore unchangeable.

This brings us to our next point—real love is *unhinderable*. That is, nothing and nobody can stop real love. The world stops loving us when we don't meet their conditions. But since there are no conditions that cause God to love us, nothing can change His mind from loving us. It's as if God is saying to us, "I love you *and there is nothing you can do to stop me!*" How beautiful is that? And that's exactly what God has always been saying.

Now I know that for many people, certain sins committed against them, especially sexual sins, make them feel dehumanized, dirty, second-class and unworthy of anyone's love. If this is true for you, please listen to what God would say, "I love you and not only is there nothing you can do to stop me, there is also *nothing anyone can do to you* to stop me from loving you!" This is why real love is unhinderable.

Finally, real love is the willingness to sacrifice self for the wellbeing of others. Jesus said,

> *Greater love has no one than this that one lay down his life for his friends.*
>
> *John 15:13*

However, real love goes even further than just loving friends. Jesus himself taught,

> *You have heard that it was said, "You shall love your neighbor and hate your enemy." But I say to you, love your enemies and pray for those who persecute you, so that you may be sons of your Father who is in heaven; for He causes His sun to rise on the evil and the good, and sends rain on the righteous and the unrighteous. For if you love those who love you, what reward do you have? Do not even the tax collectors do the same?*
>
> *Matthew 5:43-46*

The world loves those who are easy to love. However, real love is unconditional and loves everyone, including the unlovely, the enemy, the sinner, the outcast. Listen to how Paul explains God's love...

> *For while we were still helpless, at the right time Christ died for the ungodly. For one will hardly die for a righteous man; though perhaps for the good man someone would dare even to die. But God demonstrates His own love toward us, in that while we were yet sinners, Christ died for us. Much more then, having now been justified by His blood, we shall be saved from the wrath of God through Him. For if while we*

> *were enemies we were reconciled to God through the death*
> *of His Son, much more, having been reconciled, we shall be*
> *saved by His life.*
>
> *Romans 5:6-10*

There are many jewels of truth in these verses, but I would like you to focus on just a couple of them.

First, notice that God was *demonstrating* His love for us through the death of Jesus Christ. How would you know if someone really loves you? How would you know if someone is really willing to sacrifice themselves for your wellbeing? Would saying the words "I love you" be enough? Or would you be convinced of their love when they actually voluntarily give up something they need or want so you could have something you need or want? Obviously it is the latter. Love must be *demonstrated with self-sacrificing actions.*

Second, notice how God demonstrates His love for us—"Christ died for us." Look at how Paul describes the kinds of people for whom Jesus died, the people God loves: "helpless," "ungodly," "sinners" and "enemies." God does not love us because, but despite the fact that we are helpless, ungodly, sinners who have made ourselves His enemies.

> **The ultimate demonstration of God's love for us is this; Christ Jesus died for us.**

The nature of real love involves sacrifice. This is what we don't like about loving God and others. Oh, we like it when others love us and sacrifice themselves for us, but we don't want to sacrifice ourselves for others. We would rather sin.

What Is Sin?

If love is the willingness to sacrifice oneself for the well-being of others, and sin is the opposite of love, then,

> *Sin is the willingness to hurt or to sacrifice someone else for the well-being of self.*

Love sacrifices self. Sin sacrifices others. Love is other-focused. Sin is self-focused.

In short, sin is selfish. To sin is to care more about self than about God or others. I may think of you and be kind to you when it's easy or to my advantage, but when push comes to shove, if I let sin direct my choice, *I would rather hurt or neglect you than let myself be hurt.* When sin makes a choice, it will always choose self over others.

> " Sin is the willingness to hurt or to sacrifice someone else for the well-being of self. "

The Nature of Sin Is Destructive

In John 10:10, Jesus said,

> The thief comes only to steal, kill and destroy; I came that they may have life and have it abundantly.

In the context of this passage, Jesus is emphasizing His unique place as a good shepherd who will lay down His life for His sheep to save them. Now the "thief" could refer to false teachers who led the Jews astray, but humanity faces a problem much more severe than false teachers. Some have thought that the "thief" here refers to Satan. That is certainly possible. We are told that Satan, a fallen angel, cannot do anything good. The only thing Satan wants to do is to steal, kill and destroy. However, as powerful as he is, Satan is still just one fallen angel. He can't be everywhere. He's not all-powerful. And he is not our biggest problem. There is something in this world far bigger, far more powerful, far more destructive and far more universal—sin. In fact, sin is the very thing that caused Satan to become the violent creature that he is today.[3] Like a thief, sin can only do three things in your life: steal, kill and destroy.

Sin will always rob you of the good things God gives. Sin is destructive—it ruins everything it touches.

The Bible says,

> But each one is tempted when he is carried away and enticed by his own lust. Then when lust is conceived, it gives birth to sin, and when sin is accomplished, it brings forth death.
>
> *James 1:14-15*

---

3   God did not create Satan the way he is today. He was once a beautiful, holy angel. But one sin, his first sin, destroyed him, transformed him and turned him into something else.

God wove this message throughout the entire Bible. This is why God wants to stop us from sinning—sin is like poison. It will eventually kill us. Though it seems enjoyable to us, the pleasures of sin are only temporary. Ultimately, every sin can only bring one thing—death. Paul stated,

> *For the wages of sin is death...*
>
> Romans 6:23

In the Bible, the word "death" often describes a condition of brokenness. We know that something, like a phone or a watch, is broken when it doesn't work the way it was designed to. When something God created no longer works the way He designed it to, it is broken. God says it is dead. That's why Paul says,

> *If Christ is in you, though the body is dead because of sin...*
>
> Romans 8:10

Our bodies are mortal because they are damaged by sin. Becoming a Christian does not immediately fix this problem. Christians still have broken, mortal bodies—they still age and die physically. God *fixes* our broken bodies by giving us new, immortal ones in the resurrection when Jesus returns.[4] Until then, our bodies are *dead.*

Sin damages and destroys everything it touches—not just the body, but also the soul.

What Is the Soul?

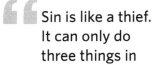

Sin is like a thief. It can only do three things in your life:
- **Steal**
- **Kill**
- **Destroy**

The human soul makes us unique from the rest of God's creation. In Genesis, God formed the first man from the dust of the ground (his physical body) and then breathed into him the breath of life. At this point it is said that Adam became a living being or *soul.*[5] The human soul was made in the image of God.

The soul is that invisible part which makes each of us a living *person*. Being a *person* in the image of God enables us to have loving relationships with others, including

4 1 Corinthians 15:51-55
5 Genesis 2:7

God Himself. Your soul enables you to think, choose and feel like God does, on a much different level compared to animals. In particular, human beings have the capacity to make moral choices and discern truth and reality in a way animals cannot.

When we open up the body, we see that it isn't made up of chocolate pudding or anything so simple. We can see that it is a miraculous work of art and engineering! If this is true of the body, it must be true of the soul as well. The soul is just as, if not more, complex and dynamic as the body. And just like the body, when one part is damaged and functions poorly, the whole soul is damaged and functions poorly.

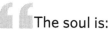

The soul is:

- **Mind**—*the capacity to think*

- **Will**—*the capacity to choose*

- **Emotions**—*the capacity to feel*

- **Personness**— *the capacity to experience loving relationships with other persons*

Sins Damage the Human Soul

It is typically easy to see when a body is damaged and why. Cuts cause bleeding, bruises cause discoloration. However, not seeing an injury doesn't mean that there is no damage. In fact, some of the most serious physical injuries, such as injuries to the brain, aren't seen on the outside at all. Sometimes the only way to know there is some damage somewhere in the body is through the evidence of pain and dysfunction.

Since we can't see the human soul, we can't see its injuries either. We must rely on the symptoms of pain and dysfunction to alert us to the existence of injury and damage. Neither can we see with our eyes what **causes** damage to the soul. To learn what kinds of things damage the soul, we must rely on God, its designer and creator, to explain it to us.

God tells us in the Bible that all sins damage the human soul and its four components.

Symptoms of a Damaged Soul

First of all, sin damages the *mind*, our capacity to think. A damaged mind is prone to believing lies, being deceived and creating its own fictitious world. God is truth, and his world is the real world, but a damaged mind finds it almost impossible to see and receive the truth. Listen to how Paul describes this:

> *So this I say, and affirm together with the Lord, that you walk no longer just as the Gentiles also walk, in the futility of their mind, being darkened in their understanding, excluded from the life of God because of the ignorance that is in them, because of the hardness of their heart.*
>
> *Ephesians 4:17-18*

"All sins damage the human soul."

A damaged mind is crippled in its ability to quickly and accurately identify and receive the truth of God. And when truth is absent, untruths are quickly received or created. This is why even Christians, indwelt by the Holy Spirit, can struggle to understand and receive God's truth. The equipment for doing so may still be unhealed and badly damaged by sin.

Second, sin damages the *will*, our capacity to choose. God designed the human soul to always choose love over sin, but a sin-damaged will can choose sin over love. This is why we always need to train ourselves to be obedient to God's directions. God always leads us in the way of truth and love, but the pressures within us, generated by a deceived mind and a damaged will, always move us towards sin.

Third, sin damages the *heart*, our capacity to feel. On the one hand, the pleasant emotions God designed for us to feel (peace, joy, satisfaction, contentment, etc.) will be hindered or altogether absent. On the other hand, emotions that God doesn't desire for us (guilt, hurt, fear, shame, worry, etc.) will become frequent, even overwhelming. We may find ourselves feeling the wrong emotion, or too much or too little of the correct emotion, for a given situation. Emotions are great indicators of what is going on inside of us—how damaged or how healed we are. We need to learn to pay attention to them and read them correctly.

Finally, sin damages our *personness*—that is, our capacity to have loving relationships with God and with others. A damaged soul will have difficulty building and maintaining loving relationships. It will seek out inappropriate relationships and damage good ones. It will also value things like experiences, power and prestige over loving relationships.

Generally, these are the symptoms we'd expect from a sin-damaged soul. But there is another very common symptom of a soul damaged by the sins of others, especially the sins of parents and older siblings.

The Two Lies of Sin

There are two lies embedded in every sin that are easily believed by a damaged soul. These two lies strike at the very heart of what it means to be human and when believed they can completely paralyze the victim. The first lie is this: ***You are not worthy of being loved.***

Since sins are the opposite of love, when someone sins against you, they are saying with their actions (which speak louder than words) that they don't really love you, not like God does. They don't see you as someone worthy of their own personal sacrifice. They see themselves as being more important and more worthy of love than you are.

This lie is very hurtful and destructive because God created human beings for love, both to receive it and to give it. All people desperately need to feel loved, and we desperately need to love others. When we feel loved and when we love others, we are feeling the very essence of life itself. We feel content, joyful and at peace. However, when a person does not feel loved they become very desperate, just like a drowning person trying to breathe.

The second lie is this: ***You are not significant.***

We also need to feel significant. God created His world such that every person has an important place in it, with roles to fulfill, projects to complete, ministries to accomplish. When a person discovers his significance to God in cooperating with Him, he feels valuable, empowered and motivated. When he doesn't feel significant, he tends to give up, pursue lesser values and compete with others, to prove to himself or others that he is significant.

It's easy for a damaged soul to believe these two lies, especially as a child. When a parent sins against a young child, the child will try to figure out why mommy or daddy hurt them. Since young children often believe mommy and daddy are perfect and can do no wrong, it's easy for them to conclude, "There must be something wrong with me. I'm not good enough. I'm not worth loving. I'm not significant." If parents never correct this by confessing their sin to their child and asking for forgiveness, the child will grow up believing these two lies. Their belief in these lies will not go away when they turn 12 or 16, get married or even when they become a Christian. I have observed people who have been Christians for decades still struggling with whether God really loves them because they cannot feel it. Oh, they know the words of truth. They can even teach it, but they cannot feel it. Why not? It is because they have a broken 'love receiver.'

Broken 'Love Receivers'

God built into the human soul the ability to feel someone's love. It acts essentially like a radio receiver. A radio station sends out invisible radio waves in all directions which we can't see or hear. A radio receiver, on the other hand, is a device that is able to receive radio waves and translate them into sounds which we can hear. If it is broken, however, it cannot do this.

Right now, radio stations are sending out radio waves all around you. You are immersed in them even as you read this book. Unless you have radio receiver turned on, however, you are completely unaware of their presence.

Similarly, God is sending out His messages of love for you continually. If sins have damaged a person's 'love receiver', he will not be able to recognize God's love—or anybody else's love for that matter. Many Christians live in this tragic condition. Being unable to feel God's love for you right now does not mean that He doesn't love you. It just means that your 'love receiver' is broken.

As we shall see later, forgiving the people who damaged our 'love receivers' allows God to heal that part of our soul. But let me be clear about this; *practicing forgiveness does not cause God to love you*. He loves you unconditionally already, and He has demonstrated that on the cross. Rather, practicing forgiveness allows God to *heal you in ways that will allow you to feel* more of His love.

Sins Damage Loving Relationships

The very first relationship that was damaged by sin was the relationship between God and man. When Adam and Eve sinned, they felt the internal damage immediately. They felt guilt, shame and fear. They felt a fear of God they had never felt before, so much so that when God came to walk with them in the garden as usual, they ran and hid themselves. Sin always damages loving relationships—first with God, and then with others.

When someone sins against you, trust is broken, fear grows, separation begins to take place and intimacy is destroyed. Security is replaced by suspicion, pleasure by irritation, anticipation by apathy or fear. You pull back, or they do, or both. The same happens when you sin against other people. In most relationships, sins are traveling in both directions, accelerating the breakdown of the relationship.

The good news is that relationships can be restored through real forgiveness. This is why the gospel of God's salvation begins with the good news of God's forgiveness through Jesus Christ. Forgiveness is the very foundation of God's work of salvation, restoring our relationship with Him. And forgiveness is the foundation for restoring broken relationships with other people too. Without forgiveness, relationships would be characterized by sin, not by love.

This means that one way we can discover sin in our lives is by looking at the *quality* of our relationships. When a relationship is not the loving relationship it could be, one or more sins (usually many sins) are the cause of the problem. At the core of every relational problem is sin—it destroys marriages, separates parents from children, causes business partnerships to fail, causes neighbors to avoid each other, causes Christians to avoid each other, causes churches to split, causes oppression and distrust between races, causes wars between nations.

If there were no sin, there would be only love, and all relationships would be harmonious and enjoyable.

The Three Paths of Sin

Sins Travel in Three Directions. We call these *the three paths of sin*.

Each path of sin is destructive in its own way. If sins are to the soul like what a knife is to the body, then when we sin against God, we are stabbing ourselves. When others sin against us, they are stabbing both us and themselves. When we sin against others, we are stabbing both them and ourselves.

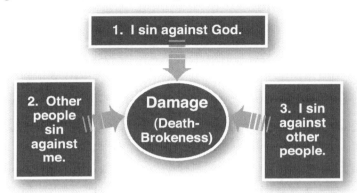

Now everyone has sinned in all these paths countless times. And if sins damage the soul, *then all of us are very wounded people*. Yes, some are much more damaged and dysfunctional than others, but everyone is broken. It's amazing that any of us can function at all—in fact, not everyone functions well. Inner brokenness is the reason why people sometimes commit horrible crimes against others or themselves. But most people find less overtly destructive ways to manage their brokenness. Let's look at some of those ways.

How Human Beings Naturally Respond to the Damage of Sin

We all have had accidents and injuries. Most of them healed completely and the adjustments that we had to make were only temporary. But perhaps you have experienced the kind of physical injury that does not heal completely or at all. Its crippling effects have hindered your strength, your freedom, your abilities, your opportunities and your health. With those kinds of injuries we have to learn to adjust our expectations and behavior permanently. We have to change the way we think, what we choose to do and how we live.

Similarly, the damage sin causes to our soul forces us to make adjustments in our lives. Most of these adjustments happen automatically—we don't even realize we are making adjustments. We are simply responding to the pain and new limitations.

Unfortunately, because we can't see the soul, we can't see the ways in which our souls have been damaged. I say "unfortunately" because most people fail to realize just how damaged they really are. If we could see the damage in our soul the way we can see a bleeding cut, we might respond differently and rush to practice forgiveness so God can heal us. However, even though we cannot see the damage in our soul, we do feel the emotional pain it causes. This is commonly felt as:

- Guilt
- Shame
- Hurt
- Bitterness
- Sorrow
- Fear
- Worry
- Anger
- Regret
- Depression

These are some of the emotions of sin.[6] They feel terrible, but really are only symptoms of damage. The emotions themselves are not the real problem— the sins that caused the damage and generated the emotions are.

When the low oil pressure light in your car comes on, the oil light is not the problem, but a symptom of a problem. The real problem is in the engine, and putting duct tape over the light doesn't fix it. Doing that would only cover up the warning sign and lead us to believe that nothing is wrong... until the problem reaches a crisis. Unfortunately, most people focus on the distressing emotions

> Painful emotions are not the problem. They are the symptom of problems located deeper in our soul.

caused by a sin rather than the sin itself. We learned as children to mask our emotions, run away from them and stuff them down deep inside. As we got older we learned to cover them up with drugs, alcohol, work, parenting, marriage, exercising, makeup, etc. Instead of practicing forgiveness we have developed *coping mechanisms*. Let's look at the following diagram to see how this process of naturally adjusting to our brokenness plays out.

6   Sometimes emotions can be generated by non-sin causes, such as allergies, chemicals, natural imbalances, fatigue and health issues, but these causes make up only a small fraction of all the emotions we feel.

The Circle of Death

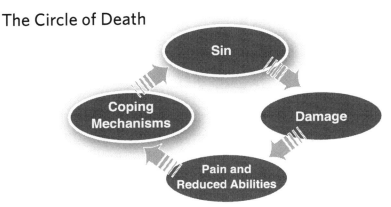

The Circle of Death begins at the top with sin, whether your own or others'. In either case any and every sin will cause damage to your soul, which you will experience in two general ways. You will feel emotional pain (one or more of the emotions of sin) and you will have reduced abilities, your soul no longer being able to do some things that you used to do. To cope with the damage, you use coping mechanisms—adjusting your thinking, your behavior and your life. Unfortunately, human coping mechanisms are not God's solution to the problem of sin. In fact, instead of solving the problem of sin, they always result in more sin, which leads to more damage... and so on and so forth. It's a deadly downward spiral.

You cannot ultimately stop sin in yourself or others—nor can you stop sins from being destructive and crippling your soul. However, *you can stop using your coping mechanisms as substitutes for real forgiveness*. That's the pathway to healing.

Our Natural Coping Mechanisms for Sin

There are at least 16 different coping mechanisms that people use to adjust to the damage of sin. All of these coping mechanisms come naturally to human beings. You yourself have experimented with all of them, even as a child. However, you have become an expert in a few of them. You found the ones that worked best for you, that were the easiest to repeat and manage. By now you have practiced the few that work best for you so many times that you have come to do them automatically, without even realizing what you are doing. They have been woven into the fabric of your personality. As you look at these coping mechanisms, pray and consider which ones you have been relying on.

In response to sin, people naturally tend to:

- *Manage their emotions*

  When people are feeling an emotion they don't like, they often try to block it out, change it, replace it or relabel it. This can be done through a variety of ways, such as a reinterpretation of the cause, denial, prayer, a change in activity or drugs.

- *Exercise self-control*

  When strong emotions push people towards destructive words or behavior, they will often try to restrain those impulses, in order to stay in control. Self-control is actually a very good thing—it is even part of what God calls "the fruit of the Spirit".[7] Exercising good self-control prevents a person from making a bad situation worse and gives people a better opportunity to practice forgiveness. However, self-control is not forgiveness and should not be used as a substitute for forgiveness.

- *Overlook sins*

  Sinning is so normal in our world that we tend to overlook sins, especially when we would consider them 'little sins'. People say: "It's just a white lie," or "Nobody's perfect," or "It's no big deal; everyone does that."

- *Misidentify sins*

  Culture, family, moral blindness and personal rebellion against God make it difficult for people to correctly identify sins. People may call something a sin when God doesn't say it is, and people may believe something is not a sin when God says it is.

- *Blame the wrong person for sins*

  Some people tend to blame themselves for others' sins, always thinking, "It's all my fault." Some tend to blame others for their own sins, thinking, "It's never my fault." Many people blame God for their sins or someone else's sin. "It's God's fault!"

---

7   Galatians 5:22-23

- *Try to forget about sins*

  If something makes them uncomfortable, many people tend to consciously or subconsciously avoid it by not thinking about it. Consciously, people can do this by always being busy, never talking about it and avoiding anything or anyone who would remind them of the sin. People may also have self-induced amnesia, blocking out the memory of a single event or period of time.

- *Minimize sins*

  We tend to compare a sin with other sins and 'grade it on a curve'. We think, "Well, this sin is not as bad as..."

- *Excuse sins*

  People tend to find reasons why certain sins are unavoidable. This is often called "situational ethics." They think that certain situations give a person no choice but to sin, and therefore, that sin is excusable. For example, someone might excuse his father's sin by thinking, "My father beat me as a child because he was raised in an abusive home himself." Understanding why a sin happened does not excuse it.

- *Justify sins*

  We tend to find reasons why certain sins were not only unavoidable, but appropriate and necessary because of the circumstances. A simple example is the cry, "He hit me first!"

- *Deny sins*

  People can deceive themselves into believing that the sin never really happened at all. This can be done deliberately by repeated self-denial, or through the brain's safety mechanism, which can bury painful memories so deep that they cannot be remembered. However, please understand - forgetting a sin doesn't mean that it didn't happen or that it didn't cause real damage to the soul.

- *Ignore sins*

  We tend to subconsciously think that if we just ignore a sin, it will go away. This is so commonly practiced by almost everyone that we don't even realize we are doing it!

- *Hide from sins*

  People tend to run away, either physically or mentally, to escape having to face sin head-on. People can use all kinds of good and bad things to hide from sin, such as work, pleasure, religion, drugs, alcohol, shopping, busyness, inactivity (isolation), sports, video games, parenting, church activities, etc. to avoid dealing with sins.

- *Tolerate sins*

  We tend to accept sins—at least a certain measure of them—as normal and inescapable, so we tolerate many sins. After all, "people are only human," and "nobody's perfect."

- *Punish someone for sins*

  People tend to try getting even—that is, to punish the guilty person. This is part of the **heart's cry for justice**, which we will discuss later.

- *Compensate for sins*

  We tend to try making up for sins by doing good things. Some may, for instance, modify their beliefs and behavior in unhealthy ways to feel like they aren't sinning, to keep themselves from sinning again or to keep others from sinning against them again.   This can lead to co-dependency and enablement.

- *"Let it go and move on"*

  We tend to try to move on and pretend that the sin doesn't affect us anymore. Many psychological tools can be used to do this—however, it's usually a combination of several of the coping mechanisms listed above.

The problem with all these coping mechanisms is that:

- None of them are true forgiveness

- None of them lead to healing

- All of them eventually lead to more sin when used as a substitute for real forgiveness

Until a person learns to practice forgiveness, he is trapped in a vicious cycle of sin and death.

Your Coping Mechanisms Don't Want to Die

Your coping mechanisms, the ones you use automatically, don't want to go away. There are strong emotional and practical reasons why you use them. They are helping you *survive*. They are helping you manage the pain and dysfunction in your life. And for the most part, you do not want to let them go because they *seem to be working for you.*

For this reason, your greatest enemy to practicing forgiveness and being healed is not Satan or other people. It's you. Nobody wants to let go of the thing they rely on for survival, no matter how bad or destructive it is, *until they find something better*. That's why an alcoholic doesn't want to stop drinking to manage his pain. That's why a self-condemning mother doesn't want to give up her self-condemnation to manage her fear of being worthless. That's why compulsive behaviors are so difficult to break.

So which coping mechanisms are you using? If you're going to practice forgiveness well, you must learn to identify your coping mechanisms and reject them. You must learn to practice real forgiveness every time you become aware of a sin in your life, instead of using your dead, useless and ineffective coping mechanisms.

At the back of this book I've included a worksheet[8] to help you uncover your automatic patterns of dealing with your sins against God, the sins others commit against you and your sins against others.

God does not want any of us to live with broken souls and broken relationships, damaged by sin. Through His gift of forgiveness, God is able to heal our soul and restore broken relationships! He can restore what sin has stolen, repair what sin has destroyed and raise to life what sin has killed. In the next chapter, we will take a closer look at how He does this.

---

8   If you need more worksheets I invite you to visit our website, www.ForgivenessMinistries.com and download the free worksheet "Identifying My Substitutes for Forgiveness" and follow the directions.

SUMMARY

- Sin damages the human soul and destroys loving relationships

- Love is the self-determined and unhinderable willingness to sacrifice self for the well-being of others

- Sin is the willingness to hurt or sacrifice others for the well-being of self

- Sin is the opposite of love

- Sin travels in three directions — we sin against God, others sin against us and we sin against others

- Time does not heal the damage caused by sin

- People automatically develop coping mechanisms that interfere with real forgiveness

CHAPTER TWO

You Can Have a Wonderful Life

The Second Key Concept of Forgiveness

Practicing all aspects of authentic forgiveness is how God heals the soul and restores relationships.

God tells us in the Bible that sin is the root of all our problems. He also tells us that we do not have the ability to fix this problem. This is an important truth to grasp because it is in our sinful nature to believe we can solve the problem of sin by ourselves, without God. We think our technology, our political structures, our financial institutions, our medical advances, our educational systems, our efforts, our religion, etc. will someday create a perfect world with perfect, immortal people.

Jesus' disciples thought they could overcome sin. So they were shocked when Jesus said,

> *"Children, how hard it is to enter the kingdom of God! It is easier for a camel to go through the eye of a needle than for a rich man to enter the kingdom of God." They were even more astonished and said to Him, "Then who can be saved?" Looking at them, Jesus said, "With people it is impossible, but not with God; for all things are possible with God."*
>
> *Mark 10:24-27*

The bad news of the Bible is not only that sin has infected and is destroying every aspect of the world, but that we humans are absolutely powerless against it. However, the 'good news' is that God loves us and that He has a solution for sin—and it begins with forgiveness.

The first and perhaps the most important truth about real forgiveness is that *forgiveness is God's idea and God's work, not man's.*

God Invented Forgiveness

Forgiveness is not a psychological trick, technique or principle that some people figured out—though many like to make it so. Humans did not come up with the idea of forgiveness, nor can we make real forgiveness happen—it is not natural to humans. (As we saw in the last chapter, we actually try to do anything and everything except real forgiveness). Authentic forgiveness is far too deep and magnificent for people to have invented it.

God did not look down on His damaged world wondering how to fix the problem of sin. At no point did He see humans practicing forgiveness and say to Himself, "Hey, that looks like a good idea. I like that;

Forgiveness is God's solution to the problem He calls sin

I think I will follow their example." Even the thought of such a scenario sounds completely absurd. God came up with the idea, and God made forgiveness possible. We learn what forgiveness is from Him.

This is extremely important because there are many ideas about forgiveness in our world today that have spawned many different ways to forgive. I have read over 60 Christian books and found in them over 30 different ways to forgive someone. Even if we don't know what real forgiveness is, I'm sure you will agree with me that God is not forgiving people in 30 different ways. In fact, since there is only one God, I'd guess that there is only one way to forgive.

You can even use this as a test to see if the way you have been taught to forgive is going to work. Look at the method that has been presented to you and ask, "Is this how God forgives?" If it isn't, then it's not really going to work. Forgiveness is from God. If we try to forgive in any way different from His way, we are going to have a difficult time. Perhaps this is why so many people find it so hard to forgive others. I'd actually take it a step further and say that if we aren't practicing forgiveness the way God does, it's not only hard, it's impossible!

True forgiveness is not only God's idea, but also God's work. God *has done something* to make forgiveness possible. During our forgiveness seminars we often ask people why God forgives us. The most common answer is, "because He loves us." Now it's absolutely true that God loves us, but God does not forgive someone simply because He loves that person.

If God could forgive us simply because He loves us, then Jesus did not need to die.

From beginning to end, the Bible emphasizes that God's forgiveness is possible only because Jesus Christ paid the penalty for our sins. Yes, it is because of God's love that He sent His Son to die for us—"For God so loved the world that He gave His one and only Son..." *(John 3:16)*—but it is what His Son did on the cross that makes forgiveness possible. As the Bible says, "without the shedding of blood,"—specifically, the blood of the perfect Son of God—"there is no forgiveness" *(Hebrews 9:22)*.

> **If God could forgive us simply because He loves us, then Jesus did not need to die.**

If Jesus did not pay that penalty, then God would be unable to forgive us, no matter how much He loves us. Now, if God is unable to forgive sins without the blood of Jesus, *then neither can we practice forgiveness effectively without the blood of Jesus.* Christians are failing to practice forgiveness well because we are trying to forgive in ways other than how God forgives.

A moment ago I mentioned that I discovered over 30 different ways to forgive from over 60 Christian books. Of those 30 ways, half do not include God in any of their steps. The next 25 percent include God, but not Jesus. The last 25 percent include Jesus, but not the Cross. If you are struggling with forgiveness, it may be because in very subtle ways, you are trying to do something God Himself cannot do.

What Forgiveness Is Not

Because of wrong ideas about forgiveness, many well-meaning people have not only become disillusioned by their practice of forgiveness, but have also often put themselves, or others, in harm's way. I would like to expose some of the most common misconceptions about forgiveness to protect you from falling into these mistakes.

✗ *Forgiveness IS NOT pretending nothing happened.* God does not forgive us by pretending that our sins didn't really happen. Nor is forgiving people accomplished by pretending that their sins didn't really happen. Denying reality is never healthy.

✗ *Forgiveness IS NOT minimizing the offense.* God does not forgive by acting as if our sins aren't as bad as they really are. In the same way, minimizing the severity of a person's sin is not forgiveness either.

✗ *Forgiveness IS NOT simply an apology.* Saying, "I'm sorry" does not necessarily acknowledge that a sin was committed and that Jesus had to die for it. Apologies are better for accidents in which no sin is involved, such as accidentally spilling hot coffee onto someone's lap. But if no sin caused the accident, then asking them to forgive you would be inappropriate. Jesus didn't die for that. However, it is appropriate to apologize and do everything you can to relieve them of the pain you caused them. In general, apologies are for accidents. Forgiveness is for sins.

35

✗ *Forgiveness IS NOT an excuse for more sin.* Being forgiven does not mean that it's okay to continue sinning or that past sins have no consequences. Nor does forgiving someone else give them permission to keep sinning against you.

✗ *Forgiveness IS NOT self-control.* Self-control is good and very important, but it's not a substitute for forgiveness.

✗ *Forgiveness IS NOT managing emotions.* Practicing forgiveness will change your emotions, but changing your emotions does not make forgiveness happen. For example, trying to get rid of anger does not produce forgiveness, but forgiving someone does cause anger to go away.

✗ *Forgiveness IS NOT a character issue.* Many people believe that God forgives because He is forgiving, and that forgiveness is a character trait. If that were true, then Jesus did not need to die for sins to make forgiveness possible. God does not forgive simply because He has a forgiving character, but because He has done something to make forgiveness possible. Similarly, we do not forgive because we become 'forgiving people', but because we believe that Jesus has paid the penalty for sins.

✗ *Forgiveness IS NOT a power issue.* In some books the author refers to the 'power' to forgive. However, power does not make forgiveness happen, and you do not need more power to practice forgiveness.

✗ *Forgiveness IS NOT a 'time' issue.* Practicing forgiveness does not require a lot of time. Real forgiveness can replace guilt and anger very quickly. It is wise to note, however, that inner healing and reconciliation through forgiveness can take time. Additionally, even when one really forgives, some sins cause such painful losses that they should be felt and grieved—such as the death of a loved one.

✗ *Forgiveness IS NOT a magic word.* Forgiveness doesn't happen just because we say the words of forgiveness—even in a prayer. Forgiveness is first a truth we need to know intimately.

✗ *Forgiveness IS NOT really even a choice.* Forgiveness does not happen because of our choice to forgive—*rather we discover that it has already happened.* This discovery makes forgiveness irresistible. However, people do need to choose to learn and practice forgiveness.

God Heals the Human Soul Through Forgiveness

When my oldest daughter Nichole was nineteen, she went on a short-term mission trip to Belize with a team from her church, including her boyfriend—now husband—Spencer. After several days of hard work the group was driven to a local river to relax, swim and cool off. Spencer knew that the locals had been diving into the river from the bridge for years. So he ran out to where he believed the water would be deep enough for a safe dive. As he dove over the guard rail he had no idea how this single act would change his life forever. Spencer's feet had not even entered the water before his head collided with one of the concrete foundations of an old bridge.

At the hospital it was discovered that Spencer had shattered a vertebrae in his neck and damaged a few others. The doctors performed surgery to try to repair the damage as best they could, but the injury left Spencer paralyzed. Today he can use his shoulders and his elbows, but not his wrists or hands. Nor can he feel or use anything below his upper chest.

Before the accident, Spencer had been an athlete in several different sports. While growing up and in high school he excelled in soccer. But now, because of his injury, he can't play soccer anymore. If a professional soccer team invited him to travel with them for a year and go to all their games, practices and coaches' meetings, and if all the players on the team taught him everything they knew about the sport, would Spencer be able to play soccer any better than he would be able to today? No. Why? Because the limiting factor in his life is not a *lack of information*. The limiting factor is his *injury*. If Spencer is ever going to play soccer again, he needs healing, not more information about how to play soccer.

This is a simple truth we can see when it comes to physical injuries. However, since we cannot see the damage that sins inflict on a human soul, we in the church tend to think that if people just had more of the right information, then they wouldn't have all of the problems they have, and their souls would function healthily. So we build our churches around sermons and lessons and books and seminars and seminaries. We use educational strategies to try fixing problems that may actually be more like physical injuries.[9]

---

9   I am not suggesting here that we should stop teaching and studying the Bible. I am only suggesting that without practicing real forgiveness, reading the Bible won't be enough to bring about full inner healing.

> **Education is the solution when the problem is ignorance.**
>
> **Healing is the solution when the problem is injury.**

Please listen carefully to what I am saying here! It is very important and also very different from how most of us have been taught.

Knowing truth is absolutely essential to the full experience of life. After all, Jesus said, "If you continue in My word, then you are truly disciples of Mine; and you will know the truth, and the truth will make you free" *(John 8:31-32)*. When people don't know what is true, they need to come to know the truth. Learning truth is the solution to the problem of ignorance.

However, injuries are a different kind of problem. The solution to an injury is not learning, but healing.

God heals the human soul when we practice real forgiveness. When more information is used as a substitute instead, people may become better educated, but they remain broken and damaged.

Jesus Emphasized the Reason Why We Need to Practice Forgiveness

Jesus often spoke about forgiveness—in the Sermon on the Mount, in the Lord's prayer and more. His disciples heard His messages on forgiveness repeatedly and struggled with them just as we do today. At one point, Peter came to Jesus with probably one of the most well-known questions in the Bible—

> *Lord, how often shall my brother sin against me and I forgive him? Up to seven times?*
>
> *Matthew 18:21*

He had heard Jesus teach about forgiving others, even our enemies. He knew the consequences of not forgiving.[10] But he was sure Jesus couldn't

10 Matthew 6:14-15

have meant that he was to forgive every person for every sin, every time, all the time.[11] Surely Jesus didn't expect him to forgive a repeat offender indefinitely! There had to be exceptions—a limit to the number of times he had to forgive the same person for the same sin. (Are you nodding your head in agreement with Peter yet?) Let's put Peter's question into words we would use—

> Jesus, how many times do I have to forgive the person who sins against me repeatedly? Please don't tell me it's more than seven times, because I don't want to forgive him at all!

Why did Peter suggest seven? Well, at that time, the Pharisees, the teachers of the Law, were telling the Jews that God expected them to forgive the same person for the same sin up to three or four times. Peter had also heard Jesus repeatedly teach, "...unless your righteousness surpasses that of the scribes and the Pharisees, you will not enter the kingdom of heaven" (Matthew 5:20). To Peter, forgiving someone was a religious act, a chore, a job needed to be done in obedience to God. He knew he had to do it, though he didn't want to. The Pharisees said four times. Jesus said it would have to be more, so Peter picked a number. "Five? Probably more. Six? Hopefully not more than seven. Seven is a lot more than four. Yes, that's good. Hopefully it's not more than seven times."

The problem with Peter's question is that it's born out of a wrong way of thinking about forgiveness. Forgiveness isn't a chore or a job that needs to be done to please God. Listen to how Jesus responded,

> I do not say to you, up to seven times, but up to seventy times seven.
>
> Matthew 18:22

---

11 Mark 11:25

490 times? Really? Is that even possible? Imagine how shocked Peter would have been to hear that. This first part of Jesus' answer would have utterly destroyed Peter's ideas about forgiveness.

Jesus often did this to people during His teachings. He had to destroy His listeners' incorrect ways of thinking to make room for the truth (and He still does this today). After shattering Peter's misconceptions regarding forgiveness, Jesus told a story in order to build a better picture of forgiveness in Peter's mind (because the answer to his question is not actually the exact number 490). Peter assumed there was a limit to the number of times he had to forgive because he misunderstood *his need to forgive.*

The story Jesus told Peter involves a king who had loaned ten thousand years' worth of wages (you can do the math) to one of his servants for investment purposes. The servant, however, lost much of the money and was unable to repay the king when the loan came due. So, according to the custom at the time, the king ordered that the man's house, belongings, family and even the man himself be sold in order to repay the debt owed to him.

When the servant heard the king's command, he panicked and begged the king for more time. Feeling compassion for the servant, the king forgave him, setting him free from his debt.

But the story doesn't end there. After being forgiven of such a massive debt, the servant went to another servant who owed him a hundred days' wages and demanded that the money be returned to him immediately. The second servant begged for more time in the same fashion the first servant had done with the king. But instead of forgiving the man as the king had forgiven him, the first servant had the man thrown in debtors' prison until the money would be returned.

Eventually the king found out about this and called him back, saying, "I forgave you all that debt... Should you not also have had mercy on your fellow employee?" The king then handed the servant over to the torturers until he was able to pay back everything he originally owed.

In conclusion, Jesus drove home this lesson on forgiveness by saying,

> *My heavenly Father will also do the same to you, if each of you*
> *does not forgive his brother from your heart.*
>
> *Matthew 18:35*

This is intense! What are we to do with this teaching on forgiveness?

First, we need to remember Peter's question. Peter asked Jesus, "How many times..." However, Jesus' story did not focus on answering Peter's question—he was asking the wrong question. Instead, Jesus was telling Peter *why* he needed to forgive.

Second, Jesus was reminding Peter that he had been forgiven. Peter's king, God himself, was compassionate to forgive even extraordinary amounts of debt—through the payment Jesus would make for his sin.

Finally, Jesus was emphasizing the terrible condition a person will find himself in when he refuses to forgive. Jesus says that the person who does not forgive will be handed over to torturers. Is God cruel? Absolutely not! Is God vindictive? No. This is not a parable about God! It's a parable about *why we need to forgive*. Jesus is saying that a person who does not forgive will find himself in a condition of pain and limited freedom.

Let's think about this.

What is the job of a torturer? It is to cause pain. And torturers work in a prison—that's where this man was. Now, what is the purpose of a prison? It is to limit the prisoner's freedom. Jesus was using an illustration that his listeners could easily understand.

Torturers cause pain. Prisons restrict freedom. This is exactly what injuries to the body *and* the soul do. Sins cause emotional pain and limit the soul's ability to function well (to think clearly and discern truth, to make good and loving choices, to feel well and to enjoy loving relationships).

Jesus is not saying that God throws people into prisons when they do not forgive—injured people are already in a prison! Jesus is not saying that God sends people to torturers to cause them pain—injured people are already in pain! Peter didn't understand this about sin. He thought that forgiving someone was a religious duty, a chore. Forgiveness is not just a moral obligation. *Practicing forgiveness is the only pathway to inner healing and freedom!*

Jesus was essentially saying, "If you want My Father to heal the damage this person's sin has caused you, if you want My Father to free you from the limitations this person's sin has brought you, then you must forgive him, not seven times, not 490 times, but every time—and there are no exceptions!" Jesus taught that God cannot heal us or set us free unless we forgive, from our hearts, the people who have sinned against us.

It's also important to notice in these verses that **forgiveness has no substitute.** Jesus didn't say, "Either forgive every time or... go to church more, or tithe, or pray, or read your Bible or sing praise songs." All these things are good and uniquely beneficial, but they cannot do what only practicing forgiveness does.

Jesus makes the same emphasis in the Sermon on the Mount—

> *You have heard that the ancients were told, 'YOU SHALL NOT COMMIT MURDER' and 'Whoever commits murder shall be liable to the court.' But I say to you that everyone who is angry with his brother shall be guilty before the court; and whoever says to his brother, 'You good-for-nothing,' shall be guilty before the supreme court; and whoever says, 'You fool,' shall be guilty enough to go into the fiery hell. Therefore if you are presenting your offering at the altar, and there remember that your brother has something against you, leave your offering there before the altar and go; first be reconciled to your brother, and then come and present your offering. Make friends quickly with your opponent at law while you are with him on the way, so that your opponent may not hand you over to the judge, and the judge to the officer, and you be thrown into prison. Truly I say to you, you will not come out of there until you have paid up the last cent.*
>
> *Matthew 5:21-26*

Anger is one of the emotions generated by sin, often a symptom of having been hurt by someone. Anger is also the emotional expression of the thought, "You hurt me and I need to see you suffer so I can feel better." This is why Jesus said that an angry person is just as guilty as a murderer. Both murder and anger come out of a desire to hurt someone for personal benefit. Then Jesus talked about two different situations where someone else is angry at us.

To understand the first situation, we need to put ourselves in the shoes of the Jewish audience. At that time, the Jews had only one altar in Jerusalem. Only men could go to the altar, and only if they were accompanied by a priest. This was as close to God—whose presence was considered to be dwelling in the Temple—as a non-priest could come. When someone

42

wanted to present an offering to God, he had to stand in line and wait his turn. Then, after a long wait (and perhaps a long journey to get to Jerusalem) he would go up to the altar with a priest to present his offering. This would be a very public, high-pressure situation—behind you would be a line of men watching you while waiting their turn, and around the altar would be other worshippers and priests, presenting their offerings as well. And Jesus said that if, at that moment when you are about to present your offering,

> **Practicing forgiveness and working to repair broken relationships is more important to God than our forms of worship**

you remember that someone is angry at you, you are to stop and excuse yourself (your priest would be shocked and try to stop you from leaving) and first try to make things right with that person! According to Jesus, then, practicing forgiveness and working to repair broken relationships is more important to God than our forms of worship, even the ones He instituted! What would that look like in our churches today if Christians followed Jesus' directions? I think it would result in a lot less 'religious activity' and a lot more forgiveness and reconciliation.

Then Jesus gave another picture. He says that we should resolve our disputes before we get to court, because if we are the guilty person, our opponent will hand us over to the judge, and we will be thrown into prison. Then He says, "You will not come out of there until you have paid up the last cent" (v. 26). That is, that when we sin against others, we will find ourselves in a prison from which we cannot leave until we do what is right, repent, ask them to forgive us and, if necessary, make restitution.

The Three Paths of Forgiveness

If we want God to heal us and set us free, then we must learn to practice forgiveness rightly. In the first chapter I stated that sin travels in three directions. Similarly, there are three paths of forgiveness, each one coinciding with one of the three paths of sin.

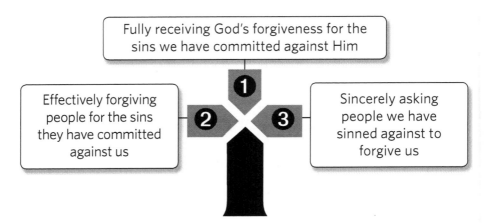

We use this picture of a cross to remind ourselves that all three paths of forgiveness are built upon what Jesus accomplished on the cross. This is why learning how to practice forgiveness must begin with a better understanding of how God forgives us. The three paths are not three different kinds of forgiveness—rather, they are three different applications of the same truths of forgiveness. If we understand forgiveness well in any one path, we will understand and be able to practice forgiveness well in the other two paths. The three paths are connected.

Many people will insist that there is a fourth path of forgiveness—self-forgiveness. But self-forgiveness is found nowhere in the Bible. It is an idea that comes from the world. Now, it does make sense that people would think that "self-forgiveness" might be the solution for self-condemnation, which is discussed in the Bible. However, self-condemnation is actually a symptom of not practicing the three paths of forgiveness well, if at all. From my observations, a person who struggles with self-condemnation isn't receiving God's forgiveness, isn't forgiving others and isn't asking others to forgive him. So the solution for self-condemnation isn't self-forgiveness, but to focus on practicing all three paths of forgiveness well.

Some might suggest that we need to forgive God. But this is also absent from the Bible. If forgiveness is a solution for sin, to talk about forgiving God is to imply that God sins. As we know, that is impossible. God never sins. However, we may at times find ourselves tremendously disappointed

> **Self-forgiveness is not the solution for self-condemnation.**

with God. We might feel that He has let us down, that He didn't rescue us when we needed to be rescued. We might even be led to believe that God is cruel and merciless. When people blame God for their pain they end up feeling angry and bitter at God.

This is tragic for two reasons. First, when we forget that God is always good and never sins, and we blame God for our pain, it prevents us from identifying the real sin(s) at the root of our pain. Instead, we need to discover what and whose sin is responsible for our pain—whether our own or others—and then practice the appropriate path of forgiveness. Second, when we blame God for our pain, our anger towards God will drive us away from Him—away from the only one who can heal us!

Each Path of Forgiveness Has Its Own Kind of Healing

God heals the human soul uniquely in each path of forgiveness. For this reason it is important that we practice the three paths in this order:

- Receiving God's forgiveness
- Forgiving other people
- Asking people to forgive us

Whenever we sin, even against another person, we are first and foremost sinning against God. We have disobeyed His command to love Him and others. So we first need to receive His forgiveness. Through this, God heals what our sin had damaged in our soul, making it possible for us to practice the second path of forgiveness. Experiencing God's love, mercy, grace and forgiveness enables us to forgive the person who has sinned against us. And when we forgive this person, God heals us and enables us to ask the other person to forgive us with more sincerity and clarity of mind. Each path of forgiveness prepares us for the next path of forgiveness, and through each path, God heals us.

When we practice forgiveness out of order, our inner brokenness hinders and can even sabotage our attempt to practice forgiveness. For instance, if we ask someone to forgive us before we have received God's forgiveness for that sin, we will be seeking from that person what only God can give us—peace and a clear conscience. People cannot give you what only God can give you. Receive His forgiveness first.

And if we ask someone to forgive us before we forgive them, our hurt and anger is going to get in the way. Instead of humbly confessing our sin to them and asking them to forgive us, we may actually be condemning them and trying to hurt them for the sins they have committed against us. Always forgive the other person before you ask them to forgive you.

Is It Too Late for You?

Upon hearing about the destructive nature of sin, many people ask me if it's too late for God to heal them. They think about the terrible things they have done, and/or the terrible things that have been done to them. They feel intense pain, anger, guilt, shame or all of the above. They feel trapped and helpless in their emotions and compulsive behaviors. Their relationships are shattered. They're alone. It feels like there is no way back, no way to God. They have been down every road they know in hope of recovery, but none have brought them any closer to healing. They've even tried forgiveness (or at least something they believed to be forgiveness). They've given up, and they believe God has given up on them.

This is my answer—It is never too late for God to heal you! Sin is strong, but God is stronger. We can't solve the problem of sin, but God can and has through forgiveness, which He has made possible through Jesus Christ. Practicing forgiveness is how God heals human souls and restores broken relationships. If you learn to practice forgiveness the way God does, He will heal your soul regardless of how damaged you are. If God can raise the dead—and He can—then He can heal your soul. God has not given up on you. Don't give up on God. No matter how tightly sin has knotted up your life, God can unravel it.

> *Now to Him who is able to do far more abundantly beyond all that we ask or think, according to the power that works within us, to Him be the glory in the church and in Christ Jesus to all generations forever and ever. Amen.*
>
> *Ephesians 3:20-21*

SUMMARY

- Education is for ignorance—healing is for injuries
- Practicing forgiveness is how God heals the human soul and restores broken relationships and there is no substitute
- Jesus Christ makes real forgiveness possible
- There are three paths of forgiveness:

    1. Receiving God's forgiveness

    2. Forgiving other people

    3. Asking other people to forgive us

- As we practice the three paths of forgiveness, we will overcome self-condemnation and resolve our anger towards God

CHAPTER THREE

The Problem of Sin Is Big

The Third Key Concept of Forgiveness

There are two sides to the problem of sin: penalty and consequences.

As I said earlier, I tried but kept failing to forgive Becky, and only found my anger growing. I realized that I didn't really know what true forgiveness is, since I couldn't do it. Desperate, I cried out to God, "Lord, what is real forgiveness and how do I do it? Please teach me." Then I turned to the Bible. I knew that whatever forgiveness was, it was something from God, and He had described it in the Bible.

Is Forgiveness Conditional or Unconditional?

As I began looking more carefully at forgiveness in the Bible, I quickly arrived at a confusing discovery. When God talks about forgiveness, sometimes it is *unconditional* and sometimes it is *conditional*.

Let's look at a few examples of this:

In 2 Chronicles 7:13-14 we read—

> *If I shut up the heavens so that there is no rain, or if I command the locust to devour the land, or if I send pestilence among My people, and My people who are called by My name humble themselves and pray and seek My face and turn from their wicked ways, then I will hear from heaven, will forgive their sin and will heal their land.*

In these verses, God tells Israel that if they:

- Humble themselves
- Pray
- Seek His face and
- Turn from their wicked ways

then He will:

- Hear from heaven
- Forgive their sins and
- Heal their land

This is a conditional statement. Conditional statements usually have two key words in them: *"if"* and *"then."* If the people of Israel who have sinned against God meet certain conditions (humble themselves, pray, seek God and repent), **then** God will respond accordingly (hear their prayers, forgive their sins and heal their land). However, if they do not meet the conditions God has set forth, then God must respond differently.

In Luke 17:3, Jesus says,

> Be on your guard! If your brother sins, rebuke him; and if he repents, forgive him.

Here we have another conditional statement about forgiveness. We are to forgive someone who has sinned against us if they repent. Jesus is also implying that *if the person who has sinned against us does not repent, then we cannot or should not forgive him.*

In Luke 24:45-47 we read—

> *Then He opened their minds to understand the Scriptures, and He said to them, "Thus it is written, that the Christ would suffer and rise again from the dead the third day, and that repentance for forgiveness of sins would be proclaimed in His name to all the nations, beginning from Jerusalem."*

These and many other verses connect forgiveness to the condition of repentance. In short, **those who repent will be forgiven, and those who do not repent will not be forgiven.**

However, Jesus also teaches that forgiveness is unconditional, as in Mark 11:25.

> *Whenever you stand praying, forgive, if you have anything against anyone...*

This is a radically *unconditional* statement about forgiveness! Let's examine it.

Jesus says, "Whenever"—that is, at any and every time—we pray and remember someone who has hurt us, we are to forgive that person. In this verse, there is no rebuking. There is no repentance. Nothing. In fact, it does not look like this person even needs to be alive. We are to forgive quickly without any conditions being met.

Jesus also says this forgiveness is to be extended to "anything" and "anyone." Which sins does the word "anything" include? Every single one of them—the serious sins and the seemingly trivial sins, the deliberate sins and the accidental sins, the persistent sins and the one-time sins. There are no sins that are unforgivable in this verse. Child abuse is forgivable. Mass murder is forgivable. Every sexual sin is forgivable. And there are no people who are unforgivable. The word "anyone" includes everyone.

Moreover, the curtness of the word "forgive" in this verse suggests that forgiveness can happen immediately and completely. It does not say "begin the process of forgiveness" or "initiate some ritual of forgiveness." It simply says "forgive." Wow! I cannot think of a more unconditional statement about forgiveness in the Bible.

Jesus has said multiple times to forgive unconditionally. But we have also seen that God forgives conditionally. Is God telling us to do something He Himself doesn't do? Or does God forgive people unconditionally too?

When we look at God's forgiveness in the New Testament it is often connected to what Jesus did on the cross. Ephesians 1:7-8 says—

> In Him we have redemption through His blood, the forgiveness
> of our trespasses, according to the riches of His grace which
> He lavished on us.

God forgives people because of the blood, the physical death of Jesus Christ. As the book of Hebrews states, "without the shedding of blood there is no forgiveness" (Hebrews 9:22). Jesus' death makes it possible for God to forgive people's sin.

In 1 John 2:2, we read—

> ...He Himself is the propitiation for our sins; and not for ours
> only, but also for those of the whole world.

What Jesus did on the Cross applies to "the whole world." This is why John the Baptist introduced Jesus with this statement. Behold, the Lamb of God who takes away the sin of the world! John 1:29

According to these verses and more, God's forgiveness of mankind is universal[12] and therefore also unconditional, since people do nothing to make it happen.

Most of the verses on forgiveness are *either* unconditional or conditional. But how can anything be both conditional and unconditional at the same time?

The solution is in a simple truth. Forgiveness is both conditional and unconditional because *there are two distinct sides to the problem of sin.*

> **"Forgiveness is both conditional and unconditional because there are two distinct sides to the problem of sin."**

A Story

It might be helpful at this point if I tell you a story.

A man wanted to kill as many people as he could, so he decided to try building an atomic bomb. However, the materials necessary to build an atomic bomb are extremely rare and highly restricted, especially the plutonium. Plutonium is a highly radioactive material controlled by the government in well-guarded facilities. Nevertheless, this man figured out how to break in and steal a significant amount of plutonium from one of these government facilities. Now he is on the run with every conceivable law enforcement agency after him. After two weeks of running he is finally captured and the plutonium is returned to its proper place.

Now, breaking into these kinds of facilities, stealing plutonium and trying to build an atomic bomb to kill people are all against the law. And because he broke the law, he must pay the penalty.

When law-makers make a new law, they must decide on the penalty for breaking that law. Laws with no penalty have no "teeth," as they say. People do not obey laws that have no penalty for non-compliance—imagine how fast people would drive if there was no penalty for driving over the speed limit. Laws must have penalties.

Since the man in our story broke several laws, he was put on trial and found guilty. The judge sentenced him according to the law—in this case,

---

12   This does not mean that everyone is saved. Salvation and forgiveness are not the same thing. Forgiveness of sins is the beginning, or the foundation, of salvation.

he is sentenced to death, and to be executed in two months. So now this man is on death row in a federal prison.

While awaiting execution, however, he begins showing symptoms of a terrible sickness. Doctors examine him and conclude that he has radiation poisoning. He has spent too much time around the plutonium without the proper protection, and now the radiation from the plutonium is killing him. The doctors have given him about two months to live.

How many problems does this man have? Some might say he has only one problem because a person can die only once. That makes sense, but let's examine the possibilities.

Let's imagine that the president of the United States decides to pardon this man of his crimes and set him free. If the president did this, how long would this man have to live? Only about two months. In this case the man will die because his very crime was a self-destructive choice. He spent too much time around highly radioactive material. Dying of radiation poisoning isn't a penalty for his crime. It is rather a consequence of his wrong choice.

Now let's look at a different ending to our story. Let's put him back on death row. The president has not pardoned him—he is still awaiting execution in two months, and he is still dying of radiation poisoning. However, doctors have discovered a possible cure for radiation poisoning and are looking for human test subjects. Our man on death row decides to volunteer. "After all," he thinks, "what have I got to lose?" So he takes the pill and within days he is cured! The radiation sickness is gone and his body is healing. In this case, how long does he have to live? Still only about two months. The government is still going to execute him as the just penalty for his crimes.

This man has two very different problems. On the one hand, the government is going to execute him to pay the just penalty for his crime. On the other hand, the consequences of his own choice are going to kill him. Both his problems will bring about his death, but for different reasons.

The same is true of sin.

The Two Sides of Sin

Every sin has two distinct problems, both of which are lethal. Every sin is a crime against God and the divine penalty for every sin is physical execution. However, every sin is also a stupid, self-destructive act that will in itself kill us. On the one hand, God must execute us for our crimes against Him. On the other hand, sin is going to kill us because it can only do three things: steal, kill, and destroy.

> **Every sin has two sides:**
> - **A divine penalty**
> - **Negative consequences**

From which problem do we need to be saved? If God saves us from only the penalty of our sins, the consequences of our sins will still kill us. If God saves us from only the consequences of our sins, God must still execute us. We need to be saved from both the penalty and the consequences of our sins.

The good news—*really the overwhelmingly great news*—is that God is willing and able to save us from both the penalty and the consequences of our sins! As is said in Hebrews 7:25, "He is able to save *to the uttermost* those who draw near to God through Him." And how He does this begins with forgiveness.

When God talks about forgiving sins, sometimes He is talking about forgiving the *penalty* for sins and sometimes He is talking about forgiving the consequences of sins.

These are the two sides of sin: penalty and consequences.

Understanding this concept is essential to understanding biblical forgiveness *because the way God forgives the penalty for sins is very different from the way God forgives the consequences of sins.* One side of forgiveness is conditional, and the other, unconditional. This is how true, biblical forgiveness can be both conditional and unconditional at the same time. It all depends on which side of sin is being forgiven.

The Consequence Side of Sin—Sin Is Always Destructive

I have already said a lot about the consequences of sin in the first chapter, but let me expand on that a little more so you can gain an even deeper understanding.

Committing a sin is like putting your hand on a hot stove. You will get burned every time—whether you do it deliberately or accidentally, once or repeatedly, voluntarily or while forced by someone else, at five or fifty years of age, being a non-Christian or a Christian. You will get burned even though God loves you and even though Jesus died to pay the penalty for those sins.

We get burned because it's in the nature of sin to destroy. Sin is destructive all the time. It doesn't matter how it gets the opportunity to destroy. As soon as someone opens the door for sin to come in, the destructive consequences begin.

Different Sins Cause Different Consequences

It's also helpful to realize that every sin has many consequences, not just one. Every sin sets in motion a chain reaction of negative consequences that touch every aspect of our lives—whether emotional, mental, physical, spiritual, relational, environmental, legal, economic, etc.

Different sins, however, trigger different consequences. We know that the consequences of stealing five dollars are different from the consequences of stealing fifty thousand dollars. We know that the consequences of hitting someone are different from the consequences of murdering someone.

Regardless of their seeming differences in severity, God calls these negative consequences "death" because they rob us of life and kill us in every way.

God Calls the Consequences of Sin "Death"

At the beginning of the Bible, God tells Adam what will happen to him if he disobeys God's warning.

> The Lord God commanded the man, saying, "From any tree of the garden you may eat freely; but from the tree of the knowledge of good and evil you shall not eat, for in the day that you eat from it you will surely die."
>
> Genesis 2:16-17

Notice that God did not say, "In the day that you eat from it I will surely kill you." Many people read Genesis 2:16-17 as a threat. It's not a threat; it's a warning born out of love.

I actually had a similar experience years ago in Hilo, Hawaii. It was absolutely gorgeous. Being a biologist, I was fascinated by all the new plants we were seeing. One day, while standing on the back porch of our host's house, I was admiring a small tree laden with huge, peach-colored flowers. The flowers were at least 10 inches long and so heavy that they hung straight down. I asked our host, standing beside me, "What are these called?" He said, "These are called Angel's Trumpet. And they are poisonous."

Concerned for our welfare, I went to my wife and our three youngest children who were with us on that trip and said, "Do not eat anything from this tree or you will get hurt, or possibly die." I wasn't threatening them, nor was our host threatening me. He was working to protect me and I was working to protect my family.

When God warned Adam about the tree of the knowledge of good and evil, there was no sin in the world—no death, no disease, no crime. The tree of the knowledge of good and evil was the doorway to sin and death.[13] God knew sin was destructive, that the tree was poisonous—but Adam didn't. So God warned Adam in love, to protect Him.

Notice, however, that when Adam and Eve disobeyed God and ate from the tree they did not immediately drop dead, even though God had said, "you will surely die." They lived many years after that. Or did they? Death takes many shapes and forms. The negative consequences of sin touch every aspect of the human experience. So if we use the word "death" the way God does, then Adam and Eve really did die immediately. Their sin damaged their souls, bodies and spirits immediately. They were no longer able to see truth clearly and always make loving choices. They saw that they were naked and felt ashamed. Their relationship with God and with each other was shattered. They ran and hid and covered themselves in fear. The environment changed; thorns and thistles began growing where only healthy, nutritious plants previously grew. They became mortal, susceptible

---

13 *Many people wonder why God put the tree in the garden in the first place if it was so poisonous. The full answer is too long to include in this book; however the tree of the knowledge of good and evil had to be in the garden so that human love could be real. Love can't be forced or manipulated. Real love must be voluntary. We must choose to love in order for our love to be real. Since God designed human beings to be able to experience the fullness of His life—the fullness of His love— He gave us the ability to choose. Not only that, He also created the opportunity for us to make a real choice. Hence the tree had to be in the garden.*

to sickness, disease and injury. They were infected with sin and they passed that disease down to their children, their children's children and so on all the way down to you and me. Oh yes, they died. They died in every way possible. Sin and death flooded into this world like an invading army.

The consequences of sin are immeasurable and inescapable. This is why God said to Adam, "You will surely die." The writer of Hebrews tells us that God's use of the word "surely" is how God swears, making an oath that these events He speaks of will come to pass.[1]. So when God said to Adam, "You will surely die," He was saying, "Adam, please do not misunderstand me. If you eat the fruit from this tree, you will most certainly die."

This was the beginning of God's warnings to mankind that all sins are destructive. This is why Jesus said of sin in Matthew 5:29-30:

> *If your right eye makes you stumble, tear it out and throw it from you; for it is better for you to lose one of the parts of your body, than for your whole body to be thrown into hell. If your right hand makes you stumble, cut it off and throw it from you; for it is better for you to lose one of the parts of your body, than for your whole body to go into hell.*

Jesus is using a very graphic, bloody picture to drive home the severity of the consequences of sin. He says that if our eye or our right hand leads us into sin, we would be better off tearing out our eye or cutting off our hand, than saving our eye or hand and suffering the eternal consequences of sin.

In Romans 6:23, Paul states—

> *For the wages of sin is death...*

I was taught that this verse refers to the penalty for sins, but it doesn't. Paul is talking about the consequences of sins. Romans 6 is all about answering the question, "Are we to continue in sin so that grace may increase?"[15] Another way of asking this question is, "Should we, believers in Jesus Christ, justified by faith in Christ, and for whom

> **God calls the consequences of sin "death."**

14 Hebrews 6:13-18
15 Romans 6:1

Jesus died and paid the penalty for our sins, keep on sinning so that God's grace through forgiveness might increase?" Paul's answer is, "May it never be," or as I like to say it, "Have you lost your mind? Absolutely not!" And Paul gives two reasons why not.

The first reason, given in the first half of Romans 6, is that we are dead to the power of sin because we have become spiritually connected to Jesus Christ. We are no longer slaves to sin. We are free to love God and to love one another. The second reason, from the second half of Romans 6, is summed up by this verse.

> *Do you not know that when you present yourselves to someone as slaves for obedience, you are slaves of the one whom you obey, either of sin resulting in death, or of obedience resulting in righteousness?*
>
> Romans 6:16

Perhaps we will understand it better if we put it in today's language. "Do you not know that you get your paycheck from the company you work for?"

If you work for the Apple Corporation, you get your paycheck from Apple. If you work for Sony, you get your paycheck from Sony. And if you work for sin, you will get your paycheck, your wages, from sin. That is, you will suffer the negative consequences of sin, "for the wages of sin is death." Many Christians believe that because God loves them, because Jesus died for them and because they are Christians, they will not have to suffer the consequences of sins. However, Paul's statement is true for Christians and for non-Christians. Remember the question Paul poses—"Are we [Christians] to continue in sin?" No. Why? First, Jesus has broken the power sin had over us. And second, when we do sin, **we will still suffer the consequences**. Why would we want to suffer the consequences of sin unnecessarily?

The Cross Does Not Change the Consequences of Sins

Many in the church, consciously or not, believe that they can sin and nothing bad will happen to them, because Jesus Christ has paid the penalty for their sins. This way of thinking existed in the early church as well. People fall into this pattern of thought when they don't understand that there are two distinct sides to sin: penalty and consequences. This is why Paul wrote,

> *Do not be deceived, God is not mocked; for whatever a man*
> *sows, this he will also reap. For the one who sows to his own*
> *flesh will from the flesh reap corruption, but the one who sows*
> *to the Spirit will from the Spirit reap eternal life.*
>
> Galatians 6:7-8

Paul uses a simple principle here, one that his audience clearly understood. The plant that grows from a seed will be the same kind of plant the seed came from. If you plant tomato seeds, you get tomato plants. If you plant thistle seeds, you get thistle plants. This biological principle is true 100 percent of the time, no exceptions. Paul is also implying that if you plant and harvest tomato seeds, you're going to have to eat tomatoes. If you plant thistle seeds, you're going to have to eat thistles. This is the law of planting and harvesting and eating.

It's interesting that Paul begins this exhortation by saying, "Do not be deceived." This means that some were in fact deceived, and that we may also be deceived in the same way.

What Paul is ultimately getting at is that sins are like seeds. When we plant the seeds of sin we will reap a harvest of "corruption" (v. 7). In Greek, this word refers to something that is decaying, falling apart or passing away. Think of something that is dead and rotting. Sins are the seed of death. On the other hand,

> **Sins were destructive before the cross of Christ. Sins are still destructive after the cross of Christ.**

when we plant the seeds of love, truth, kindness, goodness, etc. we are planting the seeds of "eternal life" (v. 8). All actions have consequences. Sin brings death. Love brings life.

The Consequences Do Not Stop With Physical Death

> *For we must all appear before the judgment seat of Christ, so*
> *that each one may be recompensed for his deeds in the body,*

> *according to what he has done, whether good or bad.*
>
> 2 Corinthians 5:10

The things we do here and now matter. For both the good and the bad things that we do and say, there are consequences now, in the future and after we die. Notice the word "recompensed," which is another way of saying "paid for what we have done." This is why Jesus encourages us in Matthew 6:18-20,

> *Do not store up for yourselves treasures on earth, where moth*
> *and rust destroy, and where thieves break in and steal. But store*
> *up for yourselves treasures in heaven, where neither moth nor*
> *rust destroys, and where thieves do not break in or steal...*

What we do now matters because we are planting seeds. Later we will reap what we sow.

How Are You Right Now?

I have to stop and ask you at this point, "How do you feel?"

I find that most people, after hearing all this about the negative consequences of sin, feel very fearful about their future. They're afraid that all the bad things they did in the past are now going to catch up to them—that there is no escape. But that isn't true. There is an escape. You don't have to suffer all the negative consequences of your sins, or the sins of others. God has made a way out. He calls it **forgiveness.**

God is able to forgive the negative consequences of sins. He forgives the negative consequences of sins when people repent. He is able to restore what sin has stolen, to fix what sin has damaged and to resurrect what sin has killed. God is renewing you! Be encouraged by this truth in Ephesians 4:22-24,

> *...in reference to your former manner of life, you lay aside the*
> *old self, which is being corrupted in accordance with the lusts*

60

*of deceit, and that you be renewed in the spirit of your mind, and put on **the new self, which in the likeness of God has been created** in righteousness and holiness of the truth.*

So do not be alarmed. Your Savior has a gift for you—the gift of forgiveness. In the next chapter, we will look at how God forgives the negative consequences of sins and how you can receive it. But first, we need to look at the other side of the problem: the penalty of sin.

The Penalty Side of Sin

In our story about the man who stole plutonium, the man is awaiting execution because he had committed a crime worthy of death. This is true of sin, too.

Every sin is a crime against God.

Every sin has a divine penalty.

The divine penalty for sin isn't because of the nature of sin. It's because of the nature of God. God is infinitely holy, righteous and just—and this makes God overwhelmingly terrifying to sinners! The Israelites themselves were overcome with fear when God appeared to them.

For you have not come to a mountain that can be touched and to a blazing fire, and to darkness and gloom and whirlwind, and to the blast of a trumpet and the sound of words which sound was such that those who heard begged that no further word be spoken to them. For they could not bear the command, "if even a beast touches the mountain, it will be stoned." And so terrible was the sight, that Moses said, "I am full of fear and trembling."

Hebrews 12:18-21

Because God is holy, righteous and just, He must take action against sin and those responsible for it. This is why God can be so terrifying to people who sin. He can't overlook sins, minimize them, excuse them, justify them or ignore them. Do these things sound familiar to you? They should. They are some of the coping mechanisms we naturally use when confronted by sin. *God cannot and will not use any of those coping mechanisms.* He must deal with sin in a holy, righteous and just manner.

God Cannot Act Unjustly

I used to be a thief. In my teenage years I was a shoplifter. I was good at it—which only means I never got caught. I stole all kinds of things—mainly tools, fishing equipment and the like—but I can still remember the first thing I stole from a store. I was in sixth grade. I was with some other boys my age in a store much like today's 7-Eleven. Some of the boys thought it would be fun to steal some candy. I didn't want to do it. I was terrified of the consequences of getting caught. That's all that I was afraid of, really. Little did I know that there were other consequences for stealing even if you didn't get caught! So, pushed by peer pressure and the need for acceptance, I joined the group and stole several packs of Razzles candy. That day changed my life for the next 15 years—and even beyond that. That day, I became a thief and a liar. I began to hurt many people in many ways.

Let me ask you—How many times do you have to steal to become a thief? If you said "once," I'd agree with you. How many times do you have to lie to become a liar? Again, only once. Now, how many times does one need to act unjustly in order to be unjust? Just once. So if God declares and demonstrates Himself to be just, how many times has God acted unjustly? That's right—never! Nor will He ever act unjustly. He can't *because He is just*; it's part of His very nature.

This tells me that whatever real forgiveness is, if God is doing it, it must be just. Forgiveness isn't ignoring or doing away with justice. This is very important because many Christians think forgiveness is doing away with justice or giving up on our need to see justice served. But this can't be true. God is just and God forgives. Somehow He has put justice and forgiveness together

What Is Justice?

Justice has something to do with balance.

If you look at the symbol of justice for the United States you will see a woman, blindfolded, holding a sword in one hand and a scale, or balance, in the other. Justice is first characterized as a woman, representing compassion. Secondly, she is blindfolded, signifying impartiality. Thirdly, she holds a scale, symbolizing balance. The idea is that crime knocks the world out of balance, weighing heavy on one end of the scale. The purpose of justice is to make the world right again, to bring things back into balance. How? By putting something on the other end of the scale, equal to the weight of the crime, to bring the world back into balance. And the woman holds a sword, conveying that someone must suffer in order to pay the penalty for the crime.

Justice has something to do with someone suffering a penalty equal to the weight of the crime.

In the Old Testament, God gave the Israelites instructions on how they were to exercise earthly, civil justice. In those directions we find some of the most well-known words in the Bible:

> *But if there is any further injury, then you shall appoint as a penalty life for life, eye for eye, tooth for tooth, hand for hand, foot for foot, burn for burn, wound for wound, bruise for bruise.*
> Exodus 21:23-25

Do you see the balance in these verses?

To us these directions seem unfathomably cruel. This is because we usually assume the people in the Bible were like ourselves, with similar value systems. However, if you went back in time and spent some time with them, you would discover that Israelites at that time were brutal and violent. For example, Genesis 34:1-29 tells us that the daughter of Jacob was raped by a man from a certain town. In retaliation, two of her brothers **killed every man in that town**. They thought this was appropriate, that this was justice. God's command was meant to restrict and control this kind of uninhibited violence towards one another in the name of "justice."

So God must exact the fair penalty for each and every sin, in order to bring about justice and bring His universe back into balance. If He doesn't, then God is no longer just, righteous or holy.

What Is the Divine Penalty for Sin?

The appropriate penalty for sin has to do with the character and nature of God Himself. All sins are crimes against God. And since God is infinitely good, infinitely holy, infinitely righteous and infinitely just, we should expect the penalty for sin to be *extremely severe*. The penalty must match the severity of the crime.

Before I suggest to you what I believe the Bible says is the appropriate penalty for sin, however, let me first ask you what you think it is. When I do this with live audiences, most people quickly shout out, "death." Then I say, "That's very good, but what kind of death?" They then shout out, "spiritual death." And I ask them, "What is spiritual death?" They rightly answer, "spiritual separation from God."

I then point out that they are correct—the Bible does talk about spiritual separation from God as spiritual death. However, I suggest to them that spiritual death isn't the penalty for sin, but rather one of the many consequences of sin.[16]

"So what are the other possibilities?" I ask them. "What are the other ways people can die?" People will then say, "eternal death." So I ask, "What is that?" And some eventually respond, "It's going to hell forever." "That's a good possibility," I tell them, "but if Jesus paid the penalty for sin, and the penalty for sin is going to hell forever, where would Jesus need to be right now?" The room gets a lot more quiet and thoughtful at this point. People then say more quietly, "I guess He would have to be in hell." I ask them is Jesus in hell. "No," they say. So going to hell forever isn't the penalty for sin either. It's another consequence of sin. More specifically, going to hell (and then to the Lake of Fire) forever is the consequence of never believing in Jesus and turning away from sin.

So I ask them, "What's left? What does the Bible say is the appropriate penalty for any and every sin?" It amazes me how quiet a room filled with Christians gets at this point. Then I prompt, "How did Jesus pay the penalty

16 The Bible teaches that spiritual separation is one of the consequences of Adam's sin. God created Adam and Eve in perfect communion with Him. However, when they sinned, that communion was broken. They became spiritually separated from God. They became spiritually dead. All their offspring are then born spiritually dead.

for our sins?" Now everyone perks up and shouts, "He died on the cross for our sins!" "That's it," I shout enthusiastically. We know what the penalty for sin is by looking at how Jesus paid the penalty. Jesus died physically to pay the penalty for our sins. **The penalty for any and every sin is physical death.**

But we need to take this further, because Jesus didn't die a normal physical death. He died in a very peculiar way—a unique way that no human being has ever died.

First of all, Jesus didn't die in an accident. Nor did He die of disease, or of old age. Jesus was executed.

Secondly, though it might look like it was the Roman soldiers who executed Jesus, Roman soldiers can't bring about *divine* justice. No human being can. And while Satan unwittingly had his hand in the crucifixion of Jesus, he is also completely unqualified to bring about divine justice. There is only one being who can bring about divine justice—God.

God is the Law-giver and the Judge. It stands to reason that He must also be the executioner. True justice is administered by God, who must exact the divine penalty for sin—physical execution by God.

This isn't so difficult to believe if we consider, if Jesus had never died for our sin in our place, what would a holy, righteous, and just God have to do to bring about divine justice? The Bible declares that God would have to execute us.

> The penalty for sin is infinitely severe because God is infinitely holy and infinitely righteous.

Is Physical Execution by God Too Severe?

What would you think if criminals were allowed to decide the penalty for their own crimes? Can you imagine how silly and tragic it would be if, after a judge pronounced someone guilty, he let the guilty person decide what penalty he should have to suffer? What a ridiculous idea! That is, however, exactly what we often do with God.

God is the Creator, the Law-giver and the Judge. When we break His laws of love, He rightly judges us and pronounces us guilty. And then we think we have the right to decide what the appropriate penalty is. We do this when we argue with the fairness of God's sentence against sin. We judge God when we believe that His sentence against sin is too severe.

Is it not logical and right for God to decide the appropriate penalty for sin? Of course it is. We are in absolutely no position to decide what's appropriate to pay the penalty for our sins. First of all, we are the guilty ones. Any judgment we make is going to be completely biased and compromised by our sin. Secondly, we are not holy. We are not righteous. We are not just. In short, we are not God!

Every Sin Has the Same Divine Penalty

Physical execution by God is the penalty for sin—*for any and every sin.* This is because every sin is like trespassing.

One of the words God uses to describe sin is "trespass." To trespass means to cross a line that shouldn't be crossed. It's often used in legal circumstances. Breaking a law is like trespassing, and trespassing is breaking the law. God uses this word to help us understand something about the singular penalty for any and every sin.

Let's imagine a square mile of land owned by a man. He builds a fence around the entire property. On each fence post, he attaches a sign that says, "No Trespassing." However, laws without penalties are meaningless. So this man goes down to the government office and is able to have a law passed stating that the fine for trespassing on this man's property is $500.

Now, what is the penalty if someone trespasses on the north side of his property? $500. What is the penalty if someone trespasses on the south side of his property? Again, it's $500. What about trespassing on the east or west sides? It's still $500. When it comes to trespassing, it doesn't matter where someone crosses the line; the penalty is the same regardless. But we aren't done yet.

> **The penalty for sins is like the penalty for trespassing. It doesn't matter where you cross the line. The penalty is always the same.**

What is the penalty if someone hops over the fence for just a minute and then hops right back? You might hesitate on your answer for this one because this episode of trespassing seems like such a small infraction. We think that perhaps it should be overlooked or the penalty altered. However, according to the law, crossing the line anywhere for any amount of time is trespassing with a penalty of $500. What if someone hops the fence, runs across the property in front of the owner's house, waves at the owner, crosses to the other side and then hops out? What is the penalty? According to the law it's still $500 for trespassing. Now pretend the far corner of this property is heavily wooded and cannot be seen from the house. What if someone climbed over the fence with all his camping equipment and lived there for three weeks? What would be the penalty? Still $500.

When it comes to trespassing, no matter where a person trespasses, how a person trespasses or how long a person trespasses, the penalty is always the same. Take a look at James 2:10-11.

> For whoever keeps the whole law and yet stumbles in one point, he has become guilty of all. For He who said, "Do not commit adultery," also said, "Do not commit murder." Now if you do not commit adultery, but do commit murder, you have become a transgressor of the law.

Here, James was asking his readers to imagine a man who has never broken any of God's laws. (There is nobody like that except Jesus, that's why we have to imagine it.) James says that if that perfect and sinless man stumbles and sins at just one point, he has broken the whole of God's law. Why? Because **there is only one God**, and this one God made all the laws (v. 11). You see, every time we sin, we trespass against God. In essence, we 'hop the fence' of God's law of love each time we sin. Just as in our story, there is one penalty no matter where, how long, or in what way we trespass.

This means that the divine penalty for rape or murder is physical execution by God. It means that the divine penalty for anger or lying is physical execution by God. And it means that the divine penalty for stealing a few packages of Razzles from a local store is physical execution by God—even if the thief is only 12 and his friends pressured him into doing it.

I imagine that a part of you is objecting to the severity of this penalty, especially for what we might call "little" sins. But remember, the guilty person doesn't get to decide on the penalty for his crime, does he?

Often people react strongly against this divine sentence for several reasons.

Firstly, we assume that the penalty for sins must follow the **same pattern** as the consequences of sins. We see that certain sins have more serious consequences while other sins have less serious consequences. To us, it seems logical that the same must be true for the divine penalty for sins. However, we do not **see** the divine penalty for sin. God must **tell** us what it is. And He tells us that the penalty for sin isn't like the consequences of sin. He tells us that the penalty for any and every sin is exactly the same—physical execution by God.

Second, we think that the severity of the divine penalty is inappropriate because it makes God look cruel, mean, unjust or unloving. But God is none of that. He is simply being completely just. God is treating every sin and every sinner according to how true justice requires Him to act to bring about balance impartially. He is treating every person and every crime exactly the same. God's love can't overrule or do away with His justice. He must always act according to His divine nature, and hence He must act justly against all sin every time. However, God is also loving and wise—He created a way by which He could act justly without destroying the person guilty of sin. But to do this, someone still had to pay the penalty. That's what Jesus came to do for us... and for God.

Third, we resist God's sentence because we have not yet seen God. The day we see God face-to-face, we will have no problem understanding the severity of sin and its penalty. Isaiah had this experience. He wrote of a rather unusual experience he had with God.

> *In the year of King Uzziah's death I saw the Lord sitting on a throne, lofty and exalted, with the train of His robe filling the temple. Seraphim stood above Him, each having six wings: with two he covered his face, and with two he covered his feet, and with two he flew. And one called out to another and said,*
>
> *"Holy, Holy, Holy, is the Lord of hosts, the whole earth is full of His glory."*
>
> *And the foundations of the thresholds trembled at the voice of him who called out, while the temple was filling with smoke.*
>
> *Then I said, "Woe is me, for I am ruined! Because I am a man of unclean lips, and I live among a people of unclean lips; for my eyes have seen the King, the Lord of hosts."*
>
> Isaiah 6:1-5

In a vision, Isaiah sees God face-to-face in His heavenly throne room. He is given this opportunity to see God because he is a prophet of God sent to speak God's word to Israel. He's not perfect, but he is following God much better than most everyone else at the time. You would think, then, that Isaiah would be overjoyed to be in God's presence. But that's not how he felt.

Isaiah was terrified. He was immediately aware of one of his sins ("I am a man of unclean lips") and he could see other people's sins more clearly ("and I live among a people of unclean lips"). Who told him this? Did some angel point out his sin when he arrived? No. *He saw his sin because he saw himself in comparison with what he saw in God*, "for my eyes have seen the King, the Lord of Hosts." Seeing God has a way of exposing sin. It also has a way of convincing us of the appropriateness of God's penalty for sins. Isaiah said, "Woe is me, for I am ruined!" In street language Isaiah was saying, "That's it. I'm dead!"

The penalty for any and every sin is the same—physical execution by God. When we see God face-to-face, this will make perfect sense. Until then, we must walk in faith, believing what God has told us. Later in Chapter 5, where we talk about how to practice forgiveness of the penalty for sins, you will see how believing this truth is instrumental to practicing forgiveness deeply and effectively.

Every sin has two sides: a divine penalty and negative consequences. The better we understand the two sides of sin, the better we understand and practice the two sides of forgiveness. The chart below will help you to quickly see the difference between the two distinct sides of the problem of sin.

A SUMMARY OF THE TWO SIDES OF SIN

THE CONSEQUENCES OF SIN	THE DIVINE PENALTY FOR SIN
The consequences of sin are what they are because of the nature of sin—sin is destructive	The divine penalty for sin is what it is because of the nature of God—God is holy, righteous and just
Every sin is a self-destructive act like putting your hand on a hot stove	Every sin is a crime against God like breaking a law
This is the natural side of sin	This is the legal side of sin
Every sin sets in motion a chain reaction of negative consequences that rob us of life	Every sin has a divine penalty
There are many different kinds of consequences depending on the sin	There is only one divine penalty for sin— physical execution by God
Without Jesus, sins would kill us	Without Jesus, God would have to execute us
We need to be saved from the consequences of sins	We need to be saved from the penalty for sins

The Bible tells us fearsome truths about sin, and yet brings good news about God's salvation from sin. Now that we have looked at the problem of sin, we are ready to look at God's solution—forgiveness.

CHAPTER FOUR

Forgiveness Is More Powerful Than Sin

The Fourth Key Concept of Forgiveness

There are two sides of forgiveness:

Personal Forgiveness and
Relational Forgiveness

Since forgiveness is God's solution for sin and since every sin has two distinct sides, it makes sense that forgiveness might also have two distinct sides that match the two sides of sin. And it does. Let's look at the two sides of biblical forgiveness.

It is very important to notice that God uses the same Hebrew and Greek words in the Bible to talk about the two sides of forgiveness. The Hebrew words which have been translated into our English word "to forgive," usually mean "to carry," "to lift," "to bear a load," and "to take away," or "to cover," and "to hide." These were ordinary words in the Hebrew language.

There are two Greek words in the Bible that have been translated into the English word "forgive" and all its derivatives. One of the Greek words means "to bestow a favor unconditionally." In our language, this word basically means "to gift." So whatever else forgiveness might be, it is a gift. This Greek word is not a religious or spiritual word. It is a common word. In the New Testament, it is translated into our word "forgive" 12 times, but 10 other times it is translated into other words focusing on the idea of a gift.

The other Greek word that has been translated as "forgiveness" is also not a religious or spiritual word. It was a very basic word, used every day in homes, business, schools, etc., which meant "to leave," "to permit," "to allow" or "to send away." In fact, it was such a common word that in the New Testament, it is translated into the English words "left," "let," "allow," "permit" or "send away" twice as often as it is translated into any form of the word "forgive."

So, using our imagination, if a Greek daughter asked her dad if she could go shopping at the Mall on Saturday, if he wanted to let her go he would *forgive* her to go, even though she had done nothing wrong. He would simply be permitting her to go.

These two words were used in all kinds of ways in different situations. The majority of those situations had nothing to do with sin. Neither the Hebrew nor the Greek language had a special word for the forgiveness of sins. This means that the Hebrew and Greek words themselves don't tell us exactly what forgiveness is, other than telling us that when God is forgiving sins He is giving us a "gift," "allowing" something, "sending away" something or "carrying" something.

Then what is He lifting, allowing or sending away? To discover this, we need to pay attention to the context in which these words are used.

The Two Sides of Forgiveness

In the last chapter I pointed out that every sin has a divine penalty and negative consequences. I suggested that when God speaks of forgiving sin, sometimes He is talking about forgiving the penalty for sins, and sometimes He is talking about forgiving the consequences of sins. I also suggested that He does these in different ways—that He forgives one unconditionally, and the other conditionally. How can we tell which side is which?

> **God forgives the penalty for a sin unconditionally because Jesus Christ has already paid the penalty for all sins.**

If we look at all the verses in the Bible, we will find that when forgiveness appears to be unconditional, it is connected to something God has already done—specifically *it is connected to the cross.* But when forgiveness is conditional, *it is usually connected to repentance.* These clues also tell us which side of sin is being forgiven—whether it is the divine penalty or the negative consequence. We will look at some of these verses, but the important truth for you to consider here is this—

> *God forgives the penalty for a sin unconditionally because Jesus Christ has already paid the penalty for that sin.*

We call this first side of forgiveness *Personal Forgiveness*. The second side of forgiveness is,

> *God forgives the consequences of a sin conditionally, that is, only if and when the guilty person repents and turns away from their sin.*

We call this *Relational Forgiveness*.

Now let me define these two sides of forgiveness a little differently, using one of the basic meanings of the main Greek word used for forgiveness. This will help you understand what God is saying when He says, "I forgive you."

- *Personal Forgiveness*

  God *sends away your need to pay the penalty* for your sins because Jesus has already paid the penalty for your sins by being executed in your place.

- *Relational Forgiveness*

  God *sends away the future negative consequences* of your sins when you repent.

Personal Forgiveness is unconditional because the basis for it has already been accomplished. God has already forgiven us because Jesus has already paid the penalty for us. Believing that Jesus has fully paid for all our sins through His death on the cross does not cause God to forgive us—rather, it allows us to experience what He has already done. Relational Forgiveness, on the other hand, is conditional because we must do something for God to forgive us of the consequences of our sins. We must repent. God cannot send away (forgive) the negative consequences of a sin unless and until we turn away from that sin.

Since the truths about forgiveness are the same whether we are receiving God's forgiveness or forgiving someone else, we can look at the second path of forgiveness—forgiving others—through the two sides of forgiveness.

- *Personal Forgiveness*

  When you believe that Jesus has already paid the penalty for someone else's sin, you will be forgiving them; you will be sending away your need to see the person who sinned against you suffer and pay the penalty for their sins.

- *Relational Forgiveness*

  You are forgiving other people when you send away (by changing them) the future negative consequences of a person's sin because they are repentant.

We call the forgiveness of the penalty for sins "Personal Forgiveness" because it is something that happens between you and God. No one can stop you from receiving God's forgiveness. It happens when you believe that Jesus Christ has fully paid the penalty for your sin and hence God has forgiven you. Neither can anyone stop you from forgiving others of the penalty for their sins. The other person doesn't need to do anything for you to forgive them of the *penalty* for their sins. They don't need to repent, to change, to ask you to forgive them, or even to be alive! When you believe that Jesus has already paid the penalty for their sins against you, and that God has forgiven them, you will experience their forgiveness!

I say "experience their forgiveness" because that is actually what happens when we forgive others of the penalty for their sins. When we forgive people, we are not really forgiving them as much as we are *discovering that God has already forgiven them*. We are entering into God's world of forgiveness through our faith, knowing that Jesus has paid for their sins as He has for us. They may not know these truths, but if you know them, they will set you free. Personal Forgiveness is about *your experience of the cross of Jesus Christ.*

Personal Forgiveness is also personal because you are the one being healed. God heals *you* when you receive His forgiveness, when you forgive someone of the penalty for their sins against you and when you sincerely ask someone to forgive you.

The second side of forgiveness, on the other hand, seeks to create the loving relationships that have been spoiled by the consequences of sin. That's why we call it "Relational Forgiveness."

> **God forgives the consequences of a sin conditionally. The condition that must be met is repentance.**

Because sin is the opposite of love, its consequences destroy loving relationships. God forgives the consequences of a sin when a person repents. When He does this He is sending away the negative consequences that would have happened if there had been no repentance—including the consequences that affect relationships. For this reason, God is able to establish a new set of positive consequences; He heals and restores broken relationships when people repent and practice Relational Forgiveness.

We need to learn how to repent and receive God's forgiveness for the consequences of our sins so that we can have a deeper, more loving relationship with Him. Similarly, we need to learn how to appropriately respond to people who truly repent of their sin against us so that, if possible, we might have a loving relationship with them. And of course, if we are to have loving relationships with others, we would need to repent of our sins against them, too.

To summarize:

- *Personal Forgiveness* is releasing a person from having to pay the penalty for their sins in light of the fact that Jesus Christ has already paid for their sins in full through His physical execution.

- *Relational Forgiveness* is reducing the negative consequences of a sin appropriate to the guilty person's level of repentance.

This is what God does when He forgives us. This is also what we need to do to forgive others. And it is the basis upon which we can ask others to forgive us.

Is this what the Bible teaches? I believe so. Let's see if these definitions work when we look at Scripture. First, let's look at verses which focus on forgiving the penalty for sins—that is, Personal Forgiveness.

Personal Forgiveness—The Forgiveness of the Penalty for Sins

Let's begin with Colossians 2:13-14.

> *When you were dead in your transgressions and the uncircumcision of your flesh, He made you alive together with Him, having forgiven us all our transgressions, having canceled out the certificate of debt consisting of decrees against us, which was hostile to us; and He has taken it out of the way, having nailed it to the cross.*

In the Roman judicial system, a judge would write out a "certificate of debt" for a criminal. This certificate of debt was a legal document that stated the crime committed, the person guilty of it and the penalty he was sentenced to. It also gave instructions to the Roman soldiers as to how they were to carry out the penalty.

This verse says that God had a "certificate of debt consisting of decrees against us" *(v. 14)*—that is, listing all our sins, all our crimes against God. Every human being has a certificate of debt with their name on it. This certificate of debt was "hostile to us" *(v. 14)*, because the penalty for our sins is that God must execute us.

When the Romans would execute someone, they would usually put a sign over the condemned person's head, stating his name and the crime for which he was being crucified. So Jesus too had a sign nailed over his head on the cross. However, all it said was, "Jesus the Nazarene, King of the Jews." The governor couldn't find any crime of which Jesus was guilty. He had sentenced Jesus to death simply to stop a riot.

However, these verses tell us that God *did* have a sign above Jesus' head on the cross, listing the crimes for which He was crucified. It was the certificate of debt for each of us. *Your certificate of debt* listing all your sins was nailed by God to Jesus' cross.

Certificates of debt were written out for all crimes, not just for those requiring execution. When a man was sentenced to five years in prison, his certificate of debt would state that penalty. After he had served his five years in prison, his certificate of debt would be brought back to a judge who would write on it, *"Paid in full."* The man would then be set free. When a condemned man was executed, the certificate of debt would be brought to the judge who would write on it, "Paid in full."

Just before Jesus died, he said, "It is finished" *(John 19:30)*—at least that's how translators have rendered the Greek word into English. (It is just one word in Greek.) However, the Greek word that Jesus said is what a Roman judge would write on a certificate of debt, "Paid in full."

When Jesus died, He paid the divine penalty for our crimes against God, so that God would write "Paid in full" on each of our certificates of debt. He has taken your certificate of debt "out of the way, having nailed it to the cross" with Jesus *(v. 14)*. He has forgiven you of the penalty for your sin—He has *sent away your need to pay for your sins*—because Jesus has already paid them for you.

The cross is how God is being both just and loving at the same time. He forgives the sinner, not executing him, but still brings about real justice by executing a willing and qualified volunteer, Jesus.

Jesus was not forced to go to the cross. He volunteered out of love for His Father and out of love for you and me.

> *For this reason the Father loves Me, because I lay down My life so that I may take it again. No one has taken it away from Me, but I lay it down on My own initiative. I have authority to lay it down, and I have authority to take it up again. This commandment I received from My Father.*
>
> *John 10:17-18*

Ephesians 1:7 says,

> *In Him we have redemption through His blood, the forgiveness of our trespasses, according to the riches of His grace...*

We see again God's forgiveness of the penalty for sins connected to the cross. "In Him," that is, Jesus, "we have redemption through His blood." To redeem something involves paying a price to buy it back. Jesus' death on the cross was the price God's love paid to God's justice in order to buy our forgiveness. Forgiveness costs God something.

In the Old Testament, God set up a system of animal sacrifices, where special animals that met rigid requirements were sacrificed every day. Of course, God wasn't really interested in animal sacrifices; rather, He was using the sacrifices as teaching tools. The lesson—something needs to die to make forgiveness of the penalty for sins possible. This is why the Bible says,

> *And according to the Law, one may almost say, all things are cleansed with blood, and without shedding of blood there is no forgiveness.*
>
> *Hebrews 9:22*

However, it also states,

> *... it is impossible for the blood of bulls and goats to take away sins.*
>
> *Hebrews 10:4*

Only a human being can pay the penalty for human sin; and only a sinless human being can pay for someone else's sins. This is why God Himself had to become a human being.

> *Therefore, He had to be made like His brethren in all things, so that He might become a merciful and faithful high priest in things pertaining to God, to make propitiation[18] for the sins of the people.*
>
> Hebrews 2:17

And,

> *Have this attitude in yourselves which was also in Christ Jesus, who, **although He existed in the form of God,** did not regard equality with God a thing to be grasped, but emptied Himself, taking the form of a bond-servant, **and being made in the likeness of men.** Being found in appearance as a man, He humbled Himself by becoming obedient to the point of death, even death on a cross.*
>
> Philippians 2:5-8

It is why we read,

> *For it was the Father's good pleasure **for all the fullness to dwell in Him** [Jesus], and through Him to reconcile all things to Himself, having made peace through the blood of His cross; through Him, I say, whether things on earth or things in heaven. And although you were formerly alienated and hostile in mind, engaged in evil deeds, yet He has now reconciled you in His fleshly body through death, in order to present you before Him holy and blameless and beyond reproach.*
>
> Colossians 1:19-22

Jesus did many things on earth—He healed the sick, cast out demons, taught, modeled real love, trained disciples, demonstrated God's love and

---

18   I will explain "propitiation" in a moment.

much more. However, the primary reason why Jesus came to earth as a human being was to die a human death. Without His death as the holy, just and righteous payment for the penalty for our sins, God would not be able to forgive us.

> For all have sinned and fall short of the glory of God, being justified as a gift by His grace through the redemption which is in Christ Jesus; whom God displayed publicly as propitiation in His blood through faith. This was to demonstrate His righteousness, because in the forbearance of God He passed over the sins previously committed; for the demonstration, I say, of His righteousness at the present time, so that He would be just and the justifier of the one who has faith in Jesus.
>
> Romans 3:23-26

Paul writes here about "being justified" (v. 24). Justification is not forgiveness, but justification is built upon forgiveness. Justification is receiving a right standing before God. God justifies those who believe in Jesus. God would not be just (v. 26) if He justified people by faith if the penalty for their sins was not paid. This is why Jesus was executed publicly, as a "demonstration" of God's "righteousness" (v. 26), which is also the Greek word for "justice." This was because in times past God had "passed over sins previously committed" (v. 25). A just and holy God should have immediately executed every human being long before Jesus. He could've executed Adam and Eve immediately after their first sin—but He didn't. He mercifully "passed over" their sins, waiting until that time when He would bring about justice against all sins at Jesus' cross.

These verses also state that Jesus' death is a "propitiation" for our sins (v. 25). A propitiation is a gift given to someone who is angry in order to appease them and take away their anger. Jesus' death was a sacrificial gift given to God, by God, to appease His just and righteous anger against all human sin.

Once, I was explaining the word "propitiation" in a forgiveness seminar. My wife Becky was in the audience. As an illustration I said that if a husband forgets his wedding anniversary, his wife will feel very hurt and very angry. When he realizes what he has done, and that his wife is angry, he will quickly run out to buy flowers, a card, some chocolate and a gift, to appease his wife's anger. These gifts, I said, would be a propitiation. At that point my wife leaned over to her girlfriend and whispered something. Both of them laughed rather loudly. Curious, I stopped the teaching to ask Becky what she had said. She answered that I still did not understand women or propitiation—that flowers, cards, chocolate and a gift would not be an adequate propitiation because that's what a husband is supposed to do when he remembers their anniversary in the first place. "Now we're talking jewelry," she said. Everyone laughed... and got the point. For a propitiation to be effective, it must have sufficient value to the one who has been offended to offset the offense.

Sin is so offensive to God that only the sacrifice of His Son can appease His holy and just anger against sin. And Paul emphasizes that it was a propitiation demonstrated publicly for all to see. The whole universe needed to see God's righteous justice against sin before He could forgive all people and justify repentant believers in Jesus.

This "demonstration" of God's justice is very important for us personally. Sin is not simply some theological idea—we feel the intense, painful reality of sin (whether our own or that of others) in our lives every day. So also we need to feel the reality of God's payment of the penalty for sins if we are going to practice forgiveness. Jesus could have paid for sins in secret. If Jesus had died for sins alone in the wilderness, instead of outside of Jerusalem, the capital city of Israel, on one of their most important national holidays, His payment would have been just as effective. However, *we would not know about it.* But because Jesus paid the penalty for sins publicly, we know for certain that God has forgiven us of the penalty for our sins. For the same reason we know for certain that Jesus has paid for everyone else's sins, so that we can forgive them, too.

Jesus Died for Every Sin

Jesus did not die just for us. He died for everyone. This is what the Bible says:

> *My little children, I am writing these things to you so that you may not sin. And if anyone sins, we have an Advocate with the Father, Jesus Christ the righteous; and He Himself is the propitiation for our sins; and not for ours only, but also for those of the whole world.*
>
> 1 John 2:1-2

Because God loves everyone, He sent His Son to pay for the sins of the entire world.

> *For God so loved the world that He gave His only begotten Son...*
>
> John 3:16

And again,

> *Behold, the Lamb of God who takes away the sin of the world!*
>
> John 1:29

This does not mean that everyone is saved. Like justification, salvation is more than being forgiven of the penalty for our sins; it also begins with and is built upon forgiveness. A person can be forgiven of the penalty for their sins, but still not be justified or saved because *every sin has two sides that can kill us*. We need to be saved from both the penalty and the consequences of our sins. Remember the man in our story who stole plutonium? He had two distinct problems. If the president pardons him of his crime, he still dies of radiation sickness. If doctors cure him, he is still executed for his crime.

"We need God to save us from both the penalty for sins and the consequences of sins."

All of humanity was on death row, awaiting execution by God as the just penalty for our sins. But, since Jesus has died for everyone's sins, God has forgiven everyone the penalty. However, every human being is dying of 'sin poisoning', as a result of the consequences of sins. God forgives people of the consequences of their sins only when they believe in Jesus and repent of their sins. When a person is forgiven of both the penalty and the consequences of their sins, they are saved. In a sense, everyone is half-saved—but half-saved is not fully saved.

Salvation is like an airplane. In order to fly, an airplane needs two wings. God has unconditionally forgiven everyone of the penalty for their sins. This is like putting one wing on an airplane. But planes cannot fly with only one wing. God gives people the second wing when they believe in Jesus, turning away from their sins.

83

Personal Forgiveness Is Unconditional and Universal

Personal Forgiveness is based upon the finished work of Jesus Christ in paying the penalty for all sins for all people. We cannot add to or take anything away from His finished work. Nor can anything we do or don't do change this historic reality. This is why the forgiveness of the penalty for sins is unconditional.

Now I know this can be very confusing for most of us. It certainly was for me. I was taught that God only forgives people *if they believe in Jesus, or when they believe in Jesus, or when they ask God to forgive them*. These are very common mindsets in the church today—however, these are not taught in the Bible. Please slowly read what I am about to say and think about it.

We have all been taught to ask God to forgive us. I have done it many times. I used to teach others to do it as well. However, the Bible does not teach that we *need* to ask God to forgive us. Now if you know your Bible, you might be thinking of two possible exceptions. The first is the Lord's Prayer.

> *Our Father who is in heaven, hallowed be Your name. Your kingdom come. Your will be done, on earth as it is in heaven. Give us this day our daily bread. And forgive us our debts, as we also have forgiven our debtors.*
>
> *Matthew 6:9–12*

The last sentence might sound like we are asking God to forgive us, but we aren't. Jesus is telling us to ask God to forgive us "just as" or "in the same way" we are forgiving others. We are actually asking God to *follow our pattern in forgiveness*. Think about this for a moment. Would you want God to forgive you in the same way you are forgiving (or not forgiving) others? Jesus put this in the prayer to get our attention and motivate us to become better forgivers.

The other possible exception is 1 John 1:9, which says,

> *If we confess our sins, He is faithful and righteous to forgive us our sins and to cleanse us from all unrighteousness.*

Here, John instructs us to confess our sins. I wholeheartedly agree! *Confession* is a part of *receiving* God's forgiveness. It does not, however, mean asking God to forgive us, nor does it make God forgive us. The Greek behind "to confess" is made up of two smaller words—one word means "same" and the other means "word." When we confess a sin, we are simply "saying the same thing" or agreeing with God about our sin.

So why doesn't the New Testament teach us to ask God to forgive us? Perhaps it's because it is unnecessary to ask someone for something they have already given you. If God has already forgiven us of the penalty for our sins because of Jesus' finished work, **we don't need to ask Him to do something He has already done!** Instead of asking for forgiveness, we ought to confess our sins, receive His forgiveness and give Him thanks for His incredible gift.

> **We do not need to ask God for something He has already given us.**

A person doesn't even need to believe in Jesus to have this gift. The Bible does say that a person needs to believe in Jesus in order to be *justified*, and to be saved from all of the consequences of sin. However, the Bible declares that God has already forgiven the *penalty* for all sins for all people, whether they believe in Jesus or not, because Jesus has already paid for all sins for all people. That's why this side of forgiveness is unconditional.

Think of it this way. Suppose a man owes his bank ten million dollars. It is due to be paid in full in two weeks, but he doesn't have the money. How do you think he is feeling? Scared? Worried? Depressed? Shamed? Yes, probably all of the above. He is in trouble.

But what if a very rich friend finds out about his problem and pays off the ten million dollars without the man even knowing about it? When would the bank cancel the man's debt? The debt would be cancelled the moment his rich friend's money was transferred into the bank. How would this man feel now? He would still feel scared, worried, depressed and shamed because *he doesn't know that his debt has been paid for*. However, if someone tells him the good news that his debt had been paid off in full and *if he believes the good news*, then he will start to feel differently.

This is exactly the situation the world is living in today. Jesus has paid off everyone's debt, but most people don't know it. They live in fear, worry, depression and shame—but they don't have to. If they only knew and believed the truth, their lives would be different. They would be filled with joy and thanksgiving. Practicing forgiveness is about knowing this truth.

> *If you continue in My word, then you are truly disciples of Mine;*
> *and you will know the truth, and the truth will make you free.*

John 8:31-32

The unconditional nature of Personal Forgiveness is also why it is a terrible sin to not forgive others of the penalty for their sins, because we are saying to God one or more of these statements:

- I don't believe that Jesus died for them.

- I don't believe that the death of Jesus was good enough to pay for their sins.

- I have a higher standard than God does.

- I don't want Jesus to pay for their sins. I want them to pay for their own sins!

All of these thoughts are terrible insults to God, who has paid such a high price to pay off everyone's debt.

A Life-changing Truth

Believing that God loves all people and that Jesus died for all people will change how you view people, including those who sin against you. Paul the apostle had this experience. Recognizing that Jesus had in fact died for everyone made Paul see all people in a different light. It compelled him to love everyone equally, as God loves them. It drove him to tell all people the wonderful news of God's forgiveness. Listen to him sharing this—

> *For the love of Christ controls us, having concluded this, that*
> *one died for all, therefore all died; and He died for all, so that*
> *they who live might no longer live for themselves, but for*
> *Him who died and rose again on their behalf. Therefore from*
> *now on we recognize no one according to the flesh; even*

86

though we have known Christ according to the flesh, yet now we know Him in this way no longer. Therefore if anyone is in Christ, he is a new creature; the old things passed away; behold, new things have come. Now all these things are from God, who reconciled us to Himself through Christ and gave us the ministry of reconciliation, namely, that God was in Christ reconciling the world to Himself, not counting their trespasses against them, and He has committed to us the word of reconciliation. Therefore, we are ambassadors for Christ, as though God were making an appeal through us; we beg you on behalf of Christ, be reconciled to God.

2 Corinthians 5:14-20

God has reconciled "the world to Himself, not counting their trespasses against them." God has released people from having to pay the penalty for their own sins because Jesus Christ has already fully paid for their sins. This is our definition of Personal Forgiveness. We are to follow His example, practicing forgiveness in the same way He has.

However, forgiveness of the penalty for sins is only the first half of biblical forgiveness. This is why Paul still exhorted his readers to "be reconciled to God." The other side of forgiveness is the forgiveness of the consequences of our sins.

Relational Forgiveness—The Forgiveness of the Consequences of Sin

When God forgives the consequences of sins, He is not sending away the sin itself or the consequences that have already happened. Both of these would require changing history. What God is sending away are the future consequences of that sin. God can do this only when the guilty person repents.

When we put our hand on a hot stove, we get burned. As long as our hand remains on the hot stove, our hand cannot heal. But when we take our hand off the hot stove, we no longer get burned, and our hand can begin to heal. Repentance changes future consequences and allows God to heal and restore. This is why forgiveness of the consequences of sins is *conditional* on people's repentance.

Hence, we define Relational Forgiveness as such:

> Relational Forgiveness is reducing the negative consequences of a sin appropriate to the guilty person's level of repentance.

God wants people to repent, but He will not force them to. Like love, repentance is a choice—so God gives people the best opportunities to repent. When they do, He saves them from the consequences of their sins. He cannot do so unless they repent.

It will be helpful for us to understand how God speaks about consequences in the Bible. In the Old Testament, God set up a special covenant, or relationship, with the Jews, in which He repeatedly told Israel that if they would listen to Him and follow Him, then good things would happen to them. But if they did not listen to God and follow Him, then bad things would happen to them.

> **Repentance is a choice—so God gives people the best opportunities to repent.**

> *Now it shall be, if you diligently obey the LORD your God, being careful to do all His commandments which I command you today, the LORD your God will set you high above all the nations of the earth. All these blessings will come upon you and overtake you if you obey the LORD your God...*
>
> *... But it shall come about, if you do not obey the LORD your God, to observe to do all His commandments and His statutes with which I charge you today, that all these curses will come upon you and overtake you...*
>
> *The LORD will send upon you curses, confusion, and rebuke, in all you undertake to do, until you are destroyed and until you perish quickly, on account of the evil of your deeds, because you have forsaken Me.*
>
> Deuteronomy 28:1-2, 15, 20 [19]

19 You can read about all the blessings and curses in Deuteronomy 28:1-20

These verses show the positive consequences of love and obedience, and the negative consequences of sin.

Since God is the Designer and Sustainer of the universe, it is true that God is burning, rightly, the person who puts their hand on a hot stove. But that's not all. God has created order and prearranged patterns for how His universe works. We see these patterns as natural rather than supernatural. So we mustn't blame God because we get burned by a hot stove. We are getting burned because in God's universe, too much heat will damage a hand. It is the natural consequence.

The great news is that God can send away these consequences by changing them when we repent! We don't need to suffer the negative consequences of sins, ours or anyone else's, forever. Sin does not have the final say in God's universe. God does.

2 Chronicles 7:13-14 tells us more about this.

> *If I shut up the heavens so that there is no rain, or if I command the locust to devour the land, or if I send pestilence among My people, and My people who are called by My name humble themselves and pray and seek My face and turn from their wicked ways, then I will hear from heaven, will forgive their sin and will heal their land.*

Whenever we see the word "forgive" in the Bible, we need to stop and ask ourselves, "Is the speaker talking about the forgiveness of the penalty or the consequences of sin—or both?" Since this verse is a conditional statement, and since there is no reference to Jesus, then this verse is about forgiving the consequences of sins. The result of this forgiveness is that God will "heal their land."

> *But when I say to the wicked, 'You will surely die,' and he turns from his sin and practices justice and righteousness, if a wicked man restores a pledge, pays back what he has taken by robbery, walks by the statutes which ensure life without committing iniquity, he shall surely live; he shall not die.*

> Ezekiel 33:14–15

When people repent, God sends away the consequences of their sin; He forgives them. John the Baptist preached this same message of repentance—

> *John the Baptist appeared in the wilderness preaching a baptism of repentance for the forgiveness of sins.*
>
> Mark 1:4

We know this verse is talking about the forgiveness of the consequences of sin, not the penalty, because **it connects forgiveness to repentance rather than the cross.**

Some think that this message of repentance was only for the people in the Old Testament—that the gospel of Christ somehow makes repentance obsolete. However, Jesus Himself said,

> *Thus it is written, that the Christ would suffer and rise again from the dead on the third day, and that repentance for forgiveness of sins would be proclaimed in His name to all the nations, beginning from Jerusalem.*
>
> Luke 24:46–47

Again, we need to ask, "Is this verse talking about forgiveness of the penalty or the consequences or both?" Though we see Christ's death in these verses, the emphasis is on repentance to make this forgiveness happen. Therefore, Jesus is talking about the forgiveness of the consequences of the repentant believer's sins. So the gospel of Christ does not make repentance obsolete—repentance is a part of the gospel. This is why Peter, after his first sermon, told his listeners,

> *Repent, and let each of you be baptized in the name of Jesus Christ for the forgiveness of your sins; and you will receive the gift of the Holy Spirit.*
>
> Acts 2:38

Here we see that repentance and belief in Jesus (exhibited by a willingness to be baptized) are the necessary conditions to receive forgiveness for the consequences of sins.

In Jesus' day, Jews assumed that a person fell sick or suffered because of their sin. Understanding this, perhaps we can look at Matthew 9:2-7 from a new perspective.

> And they brought to Him a paralytic lying on a bed. Seeing their faith, Jesus said to the paralytic, "Take courage, son; your sins are forgiven." And some of the scribes said to themselves, "This fellow blasphemes." And Jesus knowing their thoughts said, "Why are you thinking evil in your hearts? Which is easier, to say, 'Your sins are forgiven,' or to say, 'Get up, and walk?' But so that you may know that the Son of Man has authority on earth to forgive sins"—then He said to the paralytic, "Get up, pick up your bed and go home." And he got up and went home.

We don't know why this man was paralyzed, but Jesus knew what everyone was thinking: This man was paralyzed as a consequence of his sins. In this case, they might have been correct, because Jesus says to him, "Your sins are forgiven." Now, that's an easy thing to say to a paralyzed man—it's quite another thing to send away the consequences of his sin and restore his broken body. To demonstrate that He, the Son of God, has the authority to forgive the consequences of someone's sins, He heals the paralytic right before their eyes!

There are many kinds of consequences for sins—relational, economic, mental, spiritual, physical, etc. Some sicknesses are direct consequences of our own poor choices or sins. So James instructs us,

> Is anyone among you sick? Then he must call for the elders of the church and they are to pray over him, anointing him with oil in the name of the Lord; and the prayer offered in faith will restore the one who is sick, and the Lord will raise him up, and if he has committed sins, they will be forgiven him. Therefore, confess your sins to one another, and pray for one another so that you may be healed.
>
> James 5:14-16

Confession is a necessary part of repentance. When we hurt someone it isn't enough to just stop hurting them. We need to go to them and talk with them. We need to confess our sin to them. We need to take responsibility for our sin without excuses. The same is true in our relationship with God. This is the principle behind 1 John 1:9:

> *If we confess our sins, He is faithful and righteous to forgive us our sins and to cleanse us from all unrighteousness.*

This verse talks about forgiveness on the condition that we confess our sins. When we do so, God will "cleanse us from all unrighteousness," forgiving us of the consequences of our sins, changing and cleansing our condition.

Relational Forgiveness Is Like Disciplining Children

In Chapter 6 we will see that the guiding principles for Relational Forgiveness are the same as the principles for disciplining children. Sometimes children err because they don't know any better, and because at their age they may be unable to do anything different. When children disobey their parents, however, a loving parent must take action to give their child **the best opportunity to repent**. We do this for the well-being of our children.

This parallel between Relational Forgiveness and loving parental discipline will help us understand some verses about forgiveness. For example, Jesus said:

> *And that slave who knew his master's will and did not get ready or act in accord with his will, will receive many lashes, but the one who did not know it, and committed deeds worthy of a flogging, will receive but few.*
>
> Luke 12:47-48

The consequences of sins committed willingly, knowingly and deliberately are more severe than the consequences of sins committed in ignorance or under duress. This is why, after He was crucified, Jesus said:

> *Father, forgive them; for they do not know what they are doing.*
>
> Luke 23:34

Nowhere in the Bible does it say that God forgives the **penalty** for a person's sins because they "don't know what they are doing." However, sins committed in ignorance or under duress do have different consequences from sins committed deliberately.

This is what Jesus was saying about the Roman soldiers who crucified Him. Being non-Jews, they didn't know about the Messiah or the Son of God, or that Jesus might be Him. They didn't have much choice in the matter of crucifying Jesus. They were obeying orders, and if they failed to carry out those orders they would be crucified themselves. Jesus understood this. Therefore He asked His Father to treat them as children, ignorant of their sin. He asked His Father to forgive them of the consequences of their sin.

We see this when we discipline children. If a child does something wrong out of ignorance, by accident or because they were coerced by others, then the discipline we use is minimal. We don't treat a two-year-old who takes a toy from another child like we do a teenager stealing from a gas station. Nor would we discipline a five-year-old who left her coat on the playground like we would discipline a teenager who drove under the influence of alcohol. Consequences vary according to factors like age, level of willfulness or level of awareness.

In this way, Relational Forgiveness is like disciplining children—at first the consequences used to bring about repentance should be administered in the least painful way, and then only elevated when the desired goal of repentance is not attained. We see this in what is called "church discipline."

> *If your brother sins, go and show him his fault in private; if he listens to you, you have won your brother. But if he does not listen to you, take one or two more with you, so that by the mouth of two or three witnesses every fact may be confirmed. If he refuses to listen to them, tell it to the church; and if he refuses to listen even to the church, let him be to you as a Gentile and a tax collector.*
> Matthew 18:15-17

Since sins are so destructive, it is part of the loving ministry of Christians to help each other as much as possible to stop sinning. Sometimes that means going to someone and helping them see what they are doing. As with disciplining children, sometimes that is all it takes to motivate them to repent. But sometimes parents must let their children feel the painful consequences of their disobedience. Similarly, sometimes a church community must let an unrepentant member feel the painful consequences of their sin—such as withholding intimate friendship, as in this case. The Jews did not have close friendships with Gentiles (non-Jews) or tax collectors (who were considered traitors of their nation). Sometimes the only way to really love an unrepentant person is to pray for them from a distance.

Paul wrote to the Corinthian church about this very issue. Someone in the church was sinning so seriously that the church needed to exercise Relational Forgiveness and follow through with appropriate consequences. And the church discipline worked! The person became repentent. Listen to the instructions he then gives them—

> But if any has caused sorrow, he has caused sorrow not to me, but in some degree—in order not to say too much – to all of you. Sufficient for such a one is this punishment which was inflicted by the majority, so that on the contrary you should rather forgive and comfort him, otherwise such a one might be overwhelmed by excessive sorrow. Wherefore I urge you to reaffirm your love for him.
>
> 2 Corinthians 2:5-8

When a child stops disobeying, the discipline used to get them to change must either stop altogether or be adjusted. Similarly, when someone repents and wants to stop his sin, those practicing Relational Forgiveness must "forgive" and change the negative consequences they are administering. If they don't, the ongoing consequences will crush the spirit of the repentant person.

In the same letter, Paul reflects on his previous letter, which urged the Corinthians to take loving action and give the offending person the best opportunity to repent:

> For though I caused you sorrow by my letter, I do not regret it; though I did regret it—for I see that that letter caused you sorrow, though only for a while—I now rejoice, not that you were made sorrowful, but that you were made sorrowful to the point of repentance; for you were made sorrowful according to the will

of God, so that you might not suffer loss in anything through us. For the sorrow that is according to the will of God produces a repentance without regret, leading to salvation, but the sorrow of the world produces death.

2 Corinthians 7:8-10

Here, Paul lays out the principle and the purpose of repentance. He says, "you were made sorrowful to the point of repentance; for you were made sorrowful according to the will of God, so **that you might not suffer loss in anything through us.**" When we do not repent, we lose something and suffer. We miss out on experiencing the fullness of the life of God. The consequences of our sins rob us, kill us and destroy us. When we repent of our sins, however, God heals us, restores us and strengthens us.

Personal Forgiveness and Relational Forgiveness in the Same Verse

Some verses in the Bible speak about both Personal Forgiveness and Relational Forgiveness at the same time. These verses have often caused much confusion and even fear among Christians. Let me point out a couple of them and hopefully clear some of the confusion. If we read Mark 11:25 in its entirety, we hear Jesus saying,

Whenever you stand praying, forgive, if you have anything against anyone, so that your Father who is in heaven will also forgive you your transgressions.

As I previously suggested, the first half of this verse, an unconditional statement, is about the forgiveness of the penalty of sin. The second half, however, speaks about a conditional forgiveness—we must forgive in order to be forgiven. This means that Jesus is now talking about the forgiveness of the consequences of our sin. Which sin? **The sin of not forgiving people for the penalty of their sins at the cross.**

When we don't forgive those who have sinned against us, we suffer the consequences of two sins. First, we suffer the consequences of their sin against us. They forced our hand onto the hot stove; we got burned by their sin, and we continue to suffer the damage of their sin until we forgive. But if we don't forgive this person, we are also sinning against God by rejecting

95

Jesus' death as the full and just payment of the penalty for their sin. We are suffering the consequences of not forgiving them at the cross.

Another verse that speaks of both sides of forgiveness is in Matthew 6:12-15, where Jesus is commenting on a line in The Lord's Prayer.

> *"And forgive us our debts, as we also have forgiven our debtors.*
> *And do not lead us into temptation, but deliver us from evil."*
> *For if you forgive others for their transgressions, your heavenly*
> *Father will also forgive you. But if you do not forgive others,*
> *then your Father will not forgive your transgressions.*

So many people are afraid that they are going to lose (or have already lost) their salvation if they do not forgive everyone in their lives. But these verses are not about losing one's salvation—they are about suffering the consequences of the sin of unforgiveness. A saved person (justified, born again, indwelt by the Holy Spirit, etc. because of their faith and repentance) can suffer the consequences of their sins and still be a Christian. They are saved but suffering, saved but depressed, saved but angry, saved but sick. Salvation is more than forgiveness, though it is built upon it. Salvation, like forgiveness, has two sides. This is why Paul wrote,

> *For it is for this we labor and strive, because we have fixed our*
> *hope on the living God, who is the Savior of all men, especially*
> *of believers.*
>
> 1 Timothy 4:10

God is "the Savior of all men" in that He has sent His Son to save all people from the penalty of their sins. However, unless a person turns away from their sin, believing in Jesus as the only One who can save them from their sins, God cannot save them from the consequences of their sin. This is how God is the Savior "especially of believers." Only repentant believers in Jesus are forgiven of the consequences for their sins.

The Two Sides and the Three Paths of Forgiveness

Since there are two sides of forgiveness and three paths of forgiveness, there are six different applications of God's forgiveness. The simple chart below helps you to see the similarities and differences among these six applications.

PATH	PERSONAL FORGIVENESS (forgiveness of the **penalty** for sins)	RELATIONAL FORGIVENESS (forgiveness of the **consequences** of sins)
FIRST PATH Receiving God's forgiveness	We receive God's forgiveness of our sins by believing that Jesus has paid the penalty for them and that God has already forgiven us	God forgives (sends away by changing) the future consequences of our sins when we repent
SECOND PATH Forgiving other people	We forgive other people by believing that Jesus has paid the penalty for them and that God has already forgiven them	We forgive (send away by changing) the future consequences of someone's sin when they repent
THIRD PATH Asking people to forgive us	We ask others to forgive us of the penalty for our sins by helping them to focus on the death of Jesus as the payment for that sin	We ask the people we have sinned against to forgive (send away by changing) the future consequences of our sins as we demonstrate true repentance

In the next two chapters, we will learn how to practice these two sides of forgiveness in each path so that God can heal us and restore our relationships.

SUMMARY

- God forgives the divine penalty for sins because Jesus has already paid the penalty for all sins

- We call the first side of forgiveness *Personal Forgiveness*

- Personal Forgiveness is releasing a person from having to pay the penalty for their own sins in light of the fact that Jesus Christ has already paid for their sins in full through His physical execution

- God forgives the consequences of a sin when people repent

- We call the second side of forgiveness *Relational Forgiveness*

- Relational Forgiveness is reducing the negative consequences of a sin appropriate to the guilty person's level of repentance

- Forgiving the consequences of a sin means changing the future consequence, not the past

- Relational forgiveness is much like disciplining children; the consequences change according to the situation

CHAPTER FIVE

How to Practice Personal Forgiveness

The Fifth Key Concept of Forgiveness

There are six basic steps to the practice of Personal Forgiveness

K nowing about forgiveness and practicing forgiveness are two very different things. Knowing about forgiveness is like owning a bicycle. Practicing forgiveness is like riding that bicycle. Bicycles are tools for helping us get from one place to another. Having a bicycle but not riding it gets you nowhere. God designed forgiveness so you can get from where you are (broken, angry, depressed, ashamed, worried, fearful, unfulfilled, trapped, etc.) to where He wants you to be (healed, joyful, contented, free, strong, satisfied, etc.). He has given you this incredible gift of forgiveness, but you have to 'ride' it to get the wonderful life God desires that you experience together with Him. No one can do it for you. To do this we must learn how to practice Personal Forgiveness, the forgiveness of the penalty for sins.

There are six basic steps in practicing Personal Forgiveness.

These steps are not mechanical. Doing them does not make forgiveness happen. Rather, they are a way of joining with God by faith and through prayer in something He has already done. God has already forgiven you and the whole world of the penalty for sins (1 John 2:2, 2 Corinthians 5:18-19). The six steps are designed to help you follow His pattern of forgiveness so you can experience together with Him what He Himself has already experienced. Personal Forgiveness is something we do together with God.

Personal Forgiveness is also emotional. Sins bring great emotional pain not only to us, but to God as well. God's solution for sin, the cross, cost Him dearly and hurt Him deeply. We need to learn how to feel the right way towards sin, as God does. The more we do this, the closer and deeper our connection with God will be, and the deeper our forgiveness and healing will be.

For this reason, sometimes we will need to practice Personal Forgiveness together with other people. Intense emotions can overwhelm a person. God did not design human beings to endure intense emotion all alone—people can help each other through difficult sins and emotions. As you practice forgiveness, there will be times when you will need people to empathize with you, comfort you, validate you, keep you safe and keep you moving forward on the right track. This is especially true when a person is *learning* to practice forgiveness.

These six steps of Personal Forgiveness are basic steps because each step is necessary for a deep experience of forgiveness. When people tell me that forgiveness is not working for them, it's usually because they have failed to practice one or more of these basic steps well or at all. This does not mean that people must practice these six steps exactly as I outline them in order to experience real forgiveness. Many people have told me wonderful stories of how they have experienced real forgiveness without deliberately walking through these six steps. God is kind and gracious—He is able to lead people into real forgiveness even when they don't completely understand what they are doing. However, understanding how real forgiveness happens allows us to follow God's pattern deliberately and quickly. While driving, you can find your way to a new destination by wandering around, or you can use a map. Using a map usually helps people get to their destination faster. Similarly, if you know the basic steps of Personal Forgiveness, you will be able to get to your destination of healing and freedom much faster.

Before we look at the six basic steps and how they work for each path of forgiveness, let's remember our definition for Personal Forgiveness.

> **Personal Forgiveness is releasing a person from having to pay the penalty for their own sins in light of the fact that Jesus Christ has already paid for their sins in full through His physical execution.**

Here are the six basic steps of Personal Forgiveness.

Step 1. IDENTIFY the sin and the person(s) responsible for it—*see* what God sees

Step 2. FEEL the reality of the sin together with God—*feel* what God feels

Step 3: Acknowledge God's just penalty for this sin—*CONDEMN* what God condemns

Step 4. EMBRACE THE EXECUTION OF JESUS as the full and just payment for this sin—*accept* what God accepts

Step 5. COMMUNICATE with the appropriate person—speak with the person God wants you to speak with

Step 6: Let God's *LOVE* flow—*love* as God loves

To help you remember these steps, I've highlighted one word or phrase that best summarizes the step. You will want to come to know these steps by heart so you can practice them quickly, almost automatically, as soon as you discover a sin. You should deal with every sin in this way, not just the seemingly more severe ones. This needs to become a way of thinking, a way of living, so God can heal you as quickly as possible. The longer you wait to practice Personal Forgiveness, the more you will suffer unnecessarily.

Let's look at each step briefly. Afterwards, we will examine them as they apply to each of the three paths of forgiveness.

Step 1. IDENTIFY the sin and the person(s) responsible for it—see what God sees

We human beings have a very difficult time identifying sin. There are several reasons why.

Firstly, the world and everyone in it is full of sin. We see everything from a sinful human's point of view. Secondly, there is so much sin around us, we tend to overlook them as normal ("come on, nobody's perfect"). Thirdly, there are many sins we don't want to give up—so we change our standards and theology. We condemn the sins we don't want to do and justify the sins we do want to do. This is why there is so much argument about which activities are sins.

But human beings do not define sin; God does. He knows every single one of our sins, and the sins other people have committed against us. We may be blind to these sins, but He is not. If we ask Him, and if we are willing to listen, He will show us the sins in our lives in a helpful way. He will not overload us by exposing all our sins at once. (That would probably give us a heart attack!) He will reveal the next sin we need and are able to deal with at the appropriate time.

But how does God help people identify sins? How does God speak? He speaks in a variety of ways.

One of the ways God speaks is through His creation. When we look at the physical world, we see order. From the smallest subatomic particles to the largest galaxies, everything is ordered by design. Like a complex machine, each piece has a function that contributes to the effectiveness of the whole. Sometimes God reveals a sin through its dysfunctionality. Sins

103

don't fit. They cause problems—they can only "steal, kill and destroy." If something doesn't work right, it might be a sin, or the symptom of one.

Another way God speaks is through our emotions. Life and love generate emotions like peace, satisfaction, joy, security, etc. Sins generate another set of emotions: guilt, fear, worry, shame, depression, hurt, anger, bitterness, apathy, sorrow, etc. When you feel these emotions, pray. Ask God why you might be feeling what you are feeling and then listen for Him. These emotions are symptoms of sin. Track down their source. It could be one of your sins, or someone else's.

God also speaks through people—even people who don't know Him or believe in Him. When you are acting in a loving way, people will usually respond to you pleasantly. But when you sin and hurt the people around you, they will respond to you differently. They will often be very eager to tell you about your sin! Similarly, when people treat you well, others will notice it and confirm those acts of love. When people sin against you, God may use other people to point out those sins to you, especially if you are used to those sins and call them "normal." For example, people who grow up in an abusive home often believe that every home is just like theirs, and that the terrible things being done to them are normal. They don't realize that what was done to them was wrong until someone tells them. There are situations where we need an outside perspective to be able to correctly see the sins in our lives. So we need to learn to listen to others. What are people saying about how others have treated you? What are people around you saying about your own behavior?

These are three general ways in which God speaks to people about sin, but there are more. The following ways are more reliable in identifying a sin.

The clearest way God speaks to us is through the Bible.

In the Bible, God has identified many sins for us. He does this first through His commandments—rules for living—given in both the Old and New Testaments. Commandments are usually clear and straightforward.

Commandments come in two forms. Often God tells us what not to do, such as, "You shall not steal" *(Exodus 20:15)*. To do something God has commanded us not to do is called a sin of commission. Other commandments take a different form. Often God also tells us what to do, such as, "Honor your father and mother" *(Exodus 20:12)*. To not do something God has commanded us to do is called a sin of omission. When most people look for sins, they tend to focus only on sins of commission, because they are easier to see. But don't forget to look for sins of omission. These are the loving words and acts that should have been but weren't done. This is why they are more difficult to see. They never happened. They are, in a sense, invisible. Both kinds of sins are equally destructive. God's commandments can help you identify both.

However, people can sin in more ways than God enumerates through specific commands. In addition to commands, God has also given us in the Bible **principles** to guide the way we live. God's principles are broader and more general than God's commandments. Because of this, people usually debate the precise applications of these principles.

A lawyer in Jesus' day did this very thing after hearing Jesus say, "Love your neighbor as yourself" *(Luke 10:27),* which is a command in the form of a principle. He asked Jesus, "Who is my neighbor?" He wanted to avoid doing the right thing by challenging Jesus' definition of "neighbor." People do the same thing today with God's principles. In fact, I have frequently heard people say regarding this very principle, "Well, I can't love my neighbor until I first love myself." This is why God must constantly move us towards loving Him and loving others—we are all naturally focused on loving ourselves over God and others. Selfishly loving ourselves is the very foundation of sin. We all do what we think is best for ourselves. Even the person committing suicide is practicing self-love—they are doing what they think is best for themselves, no matter how it affects others. What we fail to do is love others the same way we love ourselves. By focusing on loving themselves, people excuse themselves from loving others. Use God's principles wisely to identify sins, not excuse them.

This brings me to another guideline for identifying sin, which goes back to our definition of love. Love is the self-determined and unhinderable willingness to sacrifice self for the well-being of another. Sin is the opposite of love. Sin is the willingness to sacrifice another for the well-being of self. If it is not love, then it is a sin. Sometimes simply discerning why someone is doing something will help you determine if it is a sin. When you do something for your own comfort or gain, for instance, at the expense of others, then you are sinning. Similarly, when someone is doing something for their own comfort or gain at your expense, they are sinning.

Perhaps one of the more helpful ways to identify sin is to *use Jesus as our standard for love*.

Jesus never sins. He loves God and He loves all people perfectly all the time. Jesus can be our standard for love and therefore reveal its opposite: sin. However, the effectiveness of this method is dependent on how well we know the true Jesus. All too often people imagine Jesus to be like them, approving of what they themselves approve of. So it becomes essential that we know the Jesus revealed in the Bible. The better we know the real Jesus, the easier it will be to see sin.

> **One helpful way to identify sins is to use Jesus as our standard for love.**

So when looking for sins in our lives, it can be helpful to ask these questions: Would Jesus have done what I did, or said what I said? Would Jesus have done what they did or said what they said? Would Jesus have done something different?

When we compare our behavior, or that of others, to the behavior of the real Jesus, we will find lots of sins that we wouldn't otherwise see.

Many will say that this standard is unrealistic. They say, "Nobody acts like Jesus!" And I agree. None of us come even close to being as good as Jesus. But that doesn't mean we should excuse our sins and ignore them. We need to pray and ask God for help, for Jesus to be our model for living out love.

If we are going to practice forgiveness, we must also *identify the person(s) responsible* for the sin.

Sometimes individuals sin against individuals. You are probably most familiar with these kinds of sins. However, sometimes individuals sin against groups—such as when a father sins against his family by abusing alcohol, or when an employee steals from his company. Sometimes groups sin against individuals—such as when a gang beats up a pedestrian, or when a company carelessly fires an employee to increase profits. Sometimes groups sin against groups, as we see in racial, gender or international crimes. Sometimes we may even sin against people yet to be born.[20] There is much more sin in our lives than we realize.

---

20 This is the principle behind Exodus 20:5 where God says, "You shall not worship them or serve them; for I, the LORD your God, am a jealous God, visiting the iniquity of the fathers on the children, on the third and the fourth generations of those who hate Me."

Identifying sins and who is responsible is challenging for people who are blind to sin, used to sin and excuse sin—but it is necessary. We cannot confess or forgive a sin if we don't see it as a sin. And we will not know which path of forgiveness to practice until we know who is responsible for it. Ask God to help you see what He sees—and He will.

Step 2. FEEL the reality of the sin together with God—feel what God feels

Often you will feel the reality of a sin before you identify it. Let your emotions alert you to the reality that a sin has happened. Then go look for it and identify it. At other times you will identify a sin before you feel it. When this happens, you will need to spend some extra time on this second step. This is true in all three paths of forgiveness. Practicing real forgiveness is never easy because sins cause us to feel difficult emotions we don't like. But if we are going to practice forgiveness deeply, we need to feel the emotions of our sin deeply. Otherwise, our experience of forgiveness will be shallow, and so will our healing. Even when a person knows that Jesus died for a sin, if there is little or no real emotional experience of the gravity of that sin, they will not be able to experience the forgiveness of that sin *deeply*. Whether it is our own sin or someone else's, we need to learn how to *feel* the emotional reality of that sin together with God.

I say "together with God" because that is not what we typically do. Most people learn to talk to God (by prayer), but very few learn to feel together with God. People often suffer alone—and this is a disaster. God said, "It is not good for the man to be alone" (Genesis 2:18). Human beings are not designed to live alone, and certainly not designed to suffer alone. When people suffer alone, they become very vulnerable to overwhelming pain, anguish and temptation.

The more severe the sin, the more intense the guilt, shame, fear, worry, hurt, anger, bitterness, confusion and depression are. This is why we avoid remembering our sins and the sins of others. It is just too much to bear. However, if we are going to practice forgiveness well, we must let ourselves feel these emotions again, *only this time together with God.* We need to experience emotional communion with God as we deal with these sins.

God is the Great Empathizer. He not only knows every sin in our lives, He also feels everything connected to those sins. He feels the reality of sins more deeply than we ever do since God faces sin head-on, at full strength, without running or hiding or taking pain relievers.[21]

God feels all of your hurt, anger and sorrow. God is not a robot or a machine. He is a Living Person (actually, three Persons—Father, Son and Holy Spirit). He not only feels the reality of sin indirectly through your emotions, He also feels sins directly. Since all sins are first and foremost against God, they all affect Him personally.

We need to learn to emotionally connect with God by disciplining ourselves to talk with God about our emotions *and His emotions*. God is always and has always been empathizing with us, but when we don't know or believe this, we feel neither His comfort nor His validation. We feel alone. God doesn't want you to feel alone! You have never been alone and you are not alone now. Believe that God cares about you and feels what you feel. God's Word encourages us with these words,

> *Therefore, since we have a great high priest who has passed through the heavens, Jesus the Son of God, let us hold fast our confession. For we do not have a high priest who cannot sympathize with our weaknesses, but One who has been tempted in all things as we are, yet without sin. Therefore let us draw near with confidence to the throne of grace, so that we may receive mercy and find grace to help in time of need.*
>
> Hebrews 4:14-16

While talking with and listening to God about your emotions and His emotions, you will sometimes discover that you are not feeling something He is feeling. Don't think that you are stronger than God (you are not), or that God's emotions are incorrect or unnecessary (they are correct and necessary). Rather, you will need to learn to join together with Him in what He is feeling, by paying attention to what God says in His Word and then talking with Him about it. If

---

21 In Matthew 27:33-34 the Roman soldiers who crucified Jesus gave Him something to drink with "gall" in it. Gall was a natural pain reliever. When Jesus tasted the gall, He refused to drink it, even though He was most likely desperately thirsty. God does not hide from reality or run from it, no matter how much it hurts Him.

> **God feels what you feel. He even feels it more deeply than you do.**

God feels sorrow and hurt when a person sins, then we should feel sorrow and hurt when we identify a sin. If all sins make God angry, then we also should feel angry at that sin. In fact, *the best time to forgive someone is when you are feeling the angriest at them.* And the best time to confess a sin, either to God or to another person, is when you are feeling the most sorrow for the pain you have caused to Him or others.

If you are not feeling what God feels about a particular sin, it is either because your emotional life has been paralyzed by sin, or your coping mechanism is preventing you from processing this sin adequately. When this happens, again, pray. Talk with God. Listen to Him. Ask Him to heal you so that you can feel what He feels.

Sometimes, you will need to do this step together with one or more trusted people who can empathize with, support, pray for, encourage and guide you. God is the one who loves you the most, understands the sins in your life the best and feels them the deepest. His empathy is the most powerful, but He will sometimes use other people to help us experience His love and empathy. God ministers through His people. However, as you develop a habit of practicing forgiveness, as you become more healed and feel more of God's love for you naturally, you will be able to do this step alone together with Him.

Step 3. Acknowledge God's just penalty for this sin—CONDEMN what God condemns

This step is challenging because we don't naturally accept what God says is the divine penalty for sin. However, we need to believe that what the guilty person did is worthy of death, if we are to believe and embrace that Jesus paid the penalty for sin. So many Christians fail to fully receive God's forgiveness because they don't really believe their sins are bad enough that, if not for Jesus, God would have to execute them.

You may passionately agree with God's condemnation of some sins (such as murder, abuse, etc.), but you may feel

> **How can we believe that Jesus died and paid the penalty for a sin if we don't first believe that what the guilty person did is worthy of death?**

resistant to this truth when it comes to many other sins. You may want to make excuses to minimize or justify your sin. You may want to protect a loved one from God's condemnation. Realize, however, that when you do this, you are cutting yourself off from truly believing that Jesus paid the penalty for that sin, which made forgiveness of that sin a reality. The payment for a crime must match the penalty. It simply doesn't make sense otherwise.

This truth about the divine penalty for sin is not up for public debate. We need to learn to live by faith in what He says is real and true, even though we don't yet see it. We need to learn to condemn what He condemns the way He condemns it.

Now, no one can truly see into their own heart and soul. We don't know what we really believe until a situation forces it out of us. As you practice forgiveness, you will discover what you really believe about sin. At some point, either when the sin seems small to you, or because you want to protect the guilty person, you will want to reject God's condemnation of that sin. When that happens, you will need to talk with God, remembering what His Word says about the divine penalty for any and every sin, no matter who the guilty person is. You will need to accept and trust God's Word, not your own feelings or observations.

When we look at each path of forgiveness, I will give you a way to test your faith in this truth.

Step 4. EMBRACE THE EXECUTION OF JESUS as the full and just payment for this sin—accept what God accepts

"Embrace" is a relational and emotional word. Its synonyms are: to hug, to cuddle, to squeeze, to hold close. Lovers embrace each other. Parents embrace their children. When we embrace the truth that Jesus died for us, or for someone else, we are embracing much more than a historical fact. We are embracing the heart of God Himself.

God suffered to pay the penalty for our sins. It wasn't easy. Jesus didn't just experience the agony of physical death—He also experienced God's white-hot anger against all of humanity's sins. He suffered physically, emotionally, spiritually and relationally. He who had enjoyed perfect unity with His Father from eternity past was separated from His Father for the first time. Jesus suffered in a way no human being has ever suffered.

God the Father was also suffering. He who loves His only Son was choosing to execute Him in our place, pouring out all of His holy and righteous anger on Jesus! What kind of emotional hell was He going through? And let's not forget the Spirit who was energizing this transaction so that the death of Jesus would be a real and appropriate payment for all sins. Forgiveness of the penalty for sins cost God immeasurably. God suffered in ways unimaginable to us. This is the passion of God's love for us at the cross.

The principle is this—the better we feel the heart of God at the cross, the more deeply we experience our own forgiveness, and the more quickly, fully and freely we will forgive others.

This is what I mean by "embracing the execution of Jesus as the full and just payment for this sin." We must not only understand with our head but also have our hearts touched and impacted by this truth.

Step 5. COMMUNICATE with the appropriate person—speak with the person God wants you to speak with

When someone gives you a gift it is only right to say "thank you." When you receive God's forgiveness, and when you are able to forgive someone else, you are receiving a gift. For this reason, when we are receiving God's forgiveness or forgiving someone else, it is important that we talk with God and say "thank you." Practicing forgiveness is neither only factual nor only emotional. It is also relational. We need to communicate with God.

However, when you need to ask someone you have sinned against to forgive you, you will need to ask that person.

In each case, what you say to God or to the person you sinned against will follow the pattern of the four basic steps you have just gone through. You will want to:

- Identify the sin
- Talk about how you and God feel about that sin
- Acknowledge God's just condemnation of that sin
- Focus on Jesus' death as the full and just payment for that sin

What you say next will depend on which path of forgiveness you are practicing. I will give you more help when we look at each path separately.

Step 6. Let God's LOVE flow—love as God loves

When we practice forgiveness (whether receiving it from God, forgiving someone else, or asking someone to forgive us), God begins to heal the damage those sins caused inside our soul. The way we think, act and feel will begin to change. Some of the lies we have believed will start to lose their power and attraction. Truth will take up more residence in our minds and influence us. The power behind our temptations and compulsive behaviors will decrease. Demons will have fewer opportunities to influence us. We will find ourselves desiring sin less and loving God more. More of God's love will freely flow into us and through us to others. As you practice Personal Forgiveness, God will transform you more and more into His image. The God of love will make you a person of love. Love is the fruit of real forgiveness.

> **Love is the fruit of real forgiveness.**

Experiencing more of God's love for you and through you comes naturally as a result of practicing the steps of Personal Forgiveness. However, we must also pay attention to how God wants us to actively respond to His love and deliberately love other people in new ways.

We all have ingrained coping mechanisms that created sinful habits. As we become increasingly healed, the inner pressure that pushed us into these habits decreases. But certain behaviors and thought patterns may persist because they are so natural to us. We must listen to what God says about how to think and act differently in light of our new freedom and health, much like a stroke victim might need to learn how to walk again as they recover from their stroke. Our new experiences of God's love are thus not just the fruit of practicing forgiveness, but a step in completing it.

Each path of forgiveness has its own kind of healing. The healing God gives you when you receive His forgiveness will strengthen and enable you to better forgive someone who sins against you. The healing God gives you when you forgive that person will strengthen and enable you to sincerely and honestly ask them to forgive you. *Practicing the paths of forgiveness out of order will hinder or even prevent us from practicing forgiveness well.* When someone builds a house, they first build the foundation, then the structure, and then they decorate it. Trying to decorate a house before it is built is impossible.

Trying to build a house without first laying its foundation is foolish. So it is important that we practice each path of forgiveness in the most helpful order:

1. Receive God's forgiveness
2. Forgive the other person
3. Ask that person to forgive you

We will now look at the six basic steps of Personal Forgiveness according to each path of forgiveness. First, what does it look like to receive God's forgiveness for the penalty of a sin?

First Path of Forgiveness: Receiving God's Forgiveness for the Penalty for Our Sins

Step 1. IDENTIFY your sins against God—see what God sees

To receive God's forgiveness for a particular sin in our lives, we must first identify it and admit that we are responsible for it. The best place to start is to ask God, who already knows all your sins, to show them to you. It would be helpful to pray a prayer like this,

> *Heavenly Father, please show me how I have sinned against You, how I have not loved you with my whole heart, so I can confess those sins to You, believing that Jesus has already paid the penalty for them, and receive Your forgiveness. Amen.*

Then listen for God to answer. He may show you a sin right away, or He may point something out to you later. He may speak through another person—someone who knows you well, or someone you have sinned against.

Next, we need to take a fearless moral inventory of our thoughts, words and actions. Which of God's commands and principles have you disobeyed? How have you not loved God or others? In what ways have you not been like Jesus? Whenever we haven't thought, spoken or acted like Jesus would have acted in our situation, it is likely that we have sinned against God.

When you reflect on your sins, it will be helpful to write them down. If this exercise is new to you, it may seem scary. However, as you work through Personal Forgiveness and receive His healing and freedom, you will become increasingly motivated to find as many as you can!

It is important to remember that we are also sinning against God when we sin against other people. God commands us to love one another; when we don't, we are disobeying God. Thus, when you discover a sin you have committed against someone else, *you must first deal with it as a sin against God.*

Step 2. FEEL the reality of the sin together with God— feel what God feels

Our sins affect God emotionally. They grieve and anger Him. Our sins also affect us emotionally—and they should. To ignore or deny the emotional reality of a sin is not healthy or helpful in practicing forgiveness. We need to feel God's healthy emotions together with Him when we practice forgiveness—namely, sorrow and anger.

When we discover a sin we have committed against God, we ought to feel sorrow. Feeling sorrow over causing someone pain is a healthy emotional response. Our sins hurt God. When He sees how our sins damage ourselves, others and our relationships with Him and with others, He feels just as a loving parent would feel sorrow when watching his child get hurt. The best time to confess a sin and receive forgiveness is when you are feeling most sorrowful for what you have done. Ask your loving Father how He feels about your sin, and let His sorrow guide you to a deeper sorrow of your own.

Anger is the other healthy emotion we should feel. God was once very angry at your sin, but He has exhausted His righteous anger on Jesus at the cross, and is no longer angry at you! Nevertheless, it is healthy and helpful to temporarily feel God's former anger against your sin—this will help you better understand the gravity of your sin and what it cost God to forgive you. Skipping or minimizing this step will render your practice of forgiveness shallow and weak.

The other emotions people commonly feel when they sin are guilt, shame, self-directed anger, fear and depression. These are very unhealthy and destructive, and you should avoid them.

Guilt is the emotional expression of this thought—"I did something wrong and am going to be punished for it." Guilt is the fear of punishment. However, when we believe that God isn't going to punish us for something He already punished Jesus for, the fear of punishment goes away! *Guilt is an emotion a Christian never needs to feel.*

Becoming aware of our sins may also trigger intense shame. But shame is unhealthy because shame is born out of lies. Shame is feeling unworthy of the love of God and other people, and feeling less valuable than others. These thoughts are lies. God has declared through His Word and demonstrated at the cross that you are valuable to Him. When we start to identify our sins, then, to prevent a sense of failure from resurfacing and triggering deep feelings of shame, we need to remember the truth; we are valuable to Him, not less than other people, and God loves us completely and unconditionally.

Sins carry with them a sense of failure. When someone realizes they have failed, they may feel greatly inadequate or worthless. It is also common for people to feel angry at themselves when they start looking at their own sins. We naturally get angry at whatever or whomever we believe is responsible for our pain. If you stub your toe on a chair, you might be angry at the chair, the person who moved the chair in your way or even yourself for not avoiding the chair. The problem is that *we tend to punish whatever or whomever we are angry at!* We kick the chair, yell at the person who moved it in our way or punish ourselves for doing something stupid. Overeating, giving up, sabotaging an opportunity, rebellion and abuse of alcohol or drugs are just some of the many ways people punish themselves.

When we punish ourselves we are denying the reality that Jesus was already punished in our place for our sins. Self-hatred and self-directed anger are symptoms of not yet adequately receiving God's forgiveness.

This leads to another emotion you may feel as you identify your sins— depression. Some depression is biological and natural. However, most depression is almost always a loss of hope. We've grown up in a world which strongly emphasizes that people are only valuable and worth loving if they are good enough, strong enough, pretty enough, smart enough, etc. This is why most people try so hard to be good enough, strong enough, pretty enough, smart enough—to be worthy in the eyes of others. So when we identify our sins, we may see ourselves as unworthy of love. Eventually many lose hope and fall into depression because of their failures.

> **God doesn't love us if we are good enough. He just loves us because He is love.**

However, the truth is that God loves us despite our failures! He loves us unconditionally even when others don't! We don't have to earn God's love. And there's more good news. God has the ability to change us from the inside out, making us truly loving people. We cannot make ourselves good, but He can. Our failures are only temporary. Our past does not define us. In Christ Jesus there is not only hope but a *guarantee* of this through God's promises, power and faithfulness!

> *And although you were formerly alienated and hostile in mind, engaged in evil deeds, yet He has now reconciled you in His fleshly body through death, in order to present you before Him holy and blameless and beyond reproach...*
>
> Colossians 1:21-22

You can avoid guilt, fear, shame, self-directed anger and depression by practicing forgiveness and focusing on the truths of God. Sorrow and anger, however, are emotions we need to feel together with God. Talk with God about them. Ask Him how your sin made Him feel. Join Him in His emotions, *but don't stay there*. Move on to the next step.

Step 3. Acknowledge God's just penalty for this sin— CONDEMN what God condemns

When practicing this step, ask this question aloud, "If Jesus had never come, what would a holy and just God have to do to me in order to bring about divine justice for this sin?" Then say aloud the biblical answer to this question: "Even though He loves me, God would have to execute me."

How do you feel about this answer? Does this truth make sense to you? Or do you want to reject it? If you do, why? Be very careful of letting your feelings or your limited human observations dictate what you believe. The authoritative Word of God declares that God must execute sinners in order to bring about divine justice. Do you believe this about your sin? If you do, you are ready to move on to the next step. If you don't, then you need to spend some more time meditating on what the Bible says and talking with God about this.

Step 4. EMBRACE THE EXECUTION OF JESUS as the full and just payment for this sin—accept what God accepts

Is God going to execute you for your sin? Absolutely not! He has already executed Jesus in your place for this sin. It is done. If God were to execute you for this sin, or even to punish you in some way, He would be saying to Jesus, "I've changed my mind. Your suffering and death for this sin is not enough. I want more." Can you imagine God saying that? Of course not. There is nothing you need to do to make God forgive you—He already has.

God has accepted the execution of Jesus as the full and just payment for this sin. What do you accept? What do you believe? When you believe that Jesus has paid for this sin and that God has forgiven you, you are ready for the next step.

Step 5. COMMUNICATE with the appropriate person—to God

We don't need to ask God to forgive us, since He already has, but the Bible does emphasize our need to confess our sins to God. And since forgiveness is a gift from God, we need to thank Him for it.

If I deposited a million dollars into your bank account, it would be yours, whether you knew it or not. If I told you I deposited a million dollars into your account, but you did not believe me, the money would still be yours— you simply wouldn't experience it. You would live as if the money wasn't there, even though it is. Similarly, to "receive" God's forgiveness is to believe He has already forgiven you, so that you **can experience that reality**. Believing doesn't make it happen—it opens the door to experiencing it. Believing and thanking God for His gift is how you receive it.

A good prayer of confession and thanksgiving follows the pattern of the basic steps of Personal Forgiveness. It includes:

- *Identifying the sin you are confessing to God, without excuses, taking full responsibility for what you have done*

- *Talking about how you feel about your sin and how God feels about your sin*

- *Acknowledging God's just and holy condemnation of your sin*

- *Thanking Jesus for dying to pay the penalty for this sin*

- *Thanking your Heavenly Father for forgiving you of the penalty for this sin*

- *Asking God to help you to love Him in a way that prevents you from committing this sin again*

For example, my prayer and confession of my sin of stealing candy might sound something like this:

> *Heavenly Father, thank you for showing me how I sinned against You when I stole those packages of Razzles in sixth grade. Jesus would never do that, but I did. I know this hurt You deeply because You love me, and You saw how this sin hurt me and so many others as well. I know my sin angered You. I really regret what I did. And I understand that if not for Jesus, You would have to execute me for this sin in order to bring about divine justice. However, I also know that You aren't going to execute me because You already executed Jesus in my place for my sin. Thank you, Jesus, for dying for me. Thank you for paying for this sin. Thank You, Father, for forgiving me of this sin. Now please show me how to live, trusting You, so I will not steal again. Amen.*

This is just an example. As you become familiar with the pattern, your prayers might become shorter. However, it is good to make sure you include all these important points of truth in your confession.

Confessing our sins and receiving God's forgiveness at the cross is itself an act of worship—perhaps the most important act of worship we could give God. When we receive His forgiveness, we are honoring God and the high price He paid for our forgiveness. So learn to bring every sin to God in prayer. Give God the glory, honor, thanksgiving and praise He deserves for forgiving you!

Step 6. Let God's LOVE flow—receive God's love

When a person feels like a failure, unworthy of anyone's love, they punish themselves. This includes rejecting God's love. Many people do not feel God's love, not because God doesn't love them, but because they just cannot believe it is possible for God to love them. Their 'love receivers' are broken. Practicing this first path of forgiveness opens the door for new experiences of God's love. As we confess our sins and receive God's forgiveness at the cross, we are challenged to repeatedly consider the depth of God's unconditional love for us. The more you realize how much you are forgiven and what it cost God to forgive you, the more you realize how much He must love you. Your love for Him will hence grow in response to His love for you. As Jesus said,

> *For this reason I say to you, her sins, which are many, have been forgiven, for she loved much; but he who is forgiven little, loves little.*

Luke 7:47

Second Path of Forgiveness—Forgiving People of the Penalty for Their Sins

Step 1. IDENTIFY the sins other people have committed against you—see what God sees

Just as we cannot confess a sin we haven't first identified, neither can we forgive someone of a sin we haven't yet identified. To identify the sin and who is responsible, we need God's help. God knows every sin committed against you, and who is responsible for each one. Again, the place to start is with prayer. God is faithful. When we ask, He will show us who has sinned against us and how, not so we can blame these people for our problems, rather so we can forgive them. Your prayer might sound like this:

> *Heavenly Father, who has sinned against me, and in what ways? How have people not loved me the way You do? Please show me their sins so I can forgive them just as you have forgiven me. Amen.*

Sometimes we need to make our prayer more specific in our search for sins committed by certain people in our lives:

> *Heavenly Father, how did my father/mother/spouse sin against me, and I've not yet forgiven them?*

You need to pray these kinds of prayers for everyone close to you, and then move out to friends, coworkers, classmates, neighbors, church members, etc. Some of you are thinking, "I can't do this. This will take way too much time." Healing does take time. Some sins were committed against you over long periods of time. Practicing forgiveness is not an event you do just once and it's all over just like that. Practicing forgiveness takes time. It needs to become your lifestyle, the way you live all the time.

Doctors tell us that most people don't eat well or exercise enough until they experience a heart attack and want to avoid another one. What many of them learn at that point is that they could have avoided the first heart attack if they had been eating well and exercising properly in the first place. They would also have felt better, had more strength, enjoyed more activities and been happier just by being healthier.

This principle for physical care is also true for soul care. You can spend time taking care of your soul now by doing the work of practicing forgiveness, or you can wait until you have a mental, emotional, spiritual or relational breakdown. Don't wait until you have a crisis before you spend the time finding the sins that have damaged your soul. Search them out with God's help and practice Personal Forgiveness, and many crises may NEVER happen at all. Moreover, you will experience more of the abundant life Jesus came to give you.

When you look for sins, remember that:

- *Individuals sin against individuals*
- *Individuals sin against groups*
- *Groups sin against individuals*
- *Groups sin against groups*

If we look only for sins between individuals, we will miss a lot of sins.

Again, a helpful way to discover a sin is to put Jesus in the other person's shoes and ask questions like this: "If Jesus had been my earthly father/mother/spouse/sibling/boss/neighbor/class/coach/first date, how would He have treated me differently from how they did?"

There is a lot more sin and damage in our lives than we realize. We need to take a fearless moral inventory of other people's sins against us so that we can forgive them, let God heal us and demonstrate God's glory in the cross! When we don't, we will continue suffering unnecessarily and dishonor God.

Step 2. FEEL the reality of the sin together with God— feel what God feels

When people sin against you, it's as if they are stabbing you—we should feel emotional pain. Unfortunately, many people don't feel the pain anymore. They learned to shut down their pain reflex a long time ago. It is a part of their coping mechanism. And it was a part of mine.

I learned to do this at an early age. Somehow, as a child, I learn how to "not care." If I didn't care, then people couldn't hurt me. At least, that's what I thought. I was still being damaged—I was simply blocking out the pain. I didn't start to feel the pains of sin again until I was 29. Like most men, I thought my emotional paralysis was a sign of strength. But paralysis is not a sign of strength. It's a symptom of inner damage, just as my son-in-law Spencer's paralysis is a symptom of his broken neck. If we don't feel emotional pain when people sin against us, we desperately need to practice forgiveness so God can heal our soul.

In addition to the pain, we should also feel an appropriate amount of anger. Anger is what psychologists call a "secondary emotion"—which doesn't mean a lesser emotion, but one that usually follows after another emotion. Usually, anger follows after pain. Let's go back to something I introduced previously.

Suppose you are walking through your house in the middle of the night. You catch your little toe on the leg of a chair, and suddenly feel terrible pain. What do you feel next? Most people feel anger. At what? It depends on your coping mechanism. Those who typically blame themselves for the bad things that happen will be angry at themselves.

> **Not feeling what God feels means that our emotional system is broken.**

Those who typically blame other people for their problems will get angry at the person they assume moved the chair out of place. But most people get angry at the immediate cause of their pain—the chair. So they kick the chair with their other foot. (I hope you're laughing, because it's true).

Anger is the emotional expression of this thought, "You hurt me and I need to see you suffer!" We naturally believe that if we see the person or thing that hurt us suffering, then we will feel better. That's why we kick the chair. We want to see it suffer!

Psychologists also tell us that there are two forms of anger: active anger and passive anger. Active anger sounds like this. "You hurt me. I need to see you suffer, *and I am willing to make it happen*!" It is basically revenge—the attempt to pay back the terrible thing someone did. Active anger is terrible; however, passive anger may be even worse.

Passive anger sounds like this. "You hurt me and I need to see you suffer, but... *I can't make you suffer outright*. If I do, I'll look bad or get arrested or lose my job or lose my family, etc. So I will have to wait, watch and hope." We wait and watch in hope of seeing this person suffer. When we do see this person suffer in any way—such as by finding out his mother has cancer, his spouse is having an affair, his unwed daughter is pregnant, his son just got into a car accident, etc.— outwardly we say we are so sorry for their pain, but inwardly we think, "Yes, they are finally..." What are the next words? If you said, "Getting what they deserve," you are correct. How did you know how to finish that sentence? *Because it's how we all feel.*

> **Anger is the heart's cry for justice.**

Anger is *the heart's cry for justice.*

When people hurt us, our hearts cry out for justice—and not just any human justice. That's why the family members of victims of violent crime typically don't feel satisfied even after learning of or watching the execution of the criminal. What we need to see and feel is *divine justice*, and that only happens at the cross.

We should feel pain and anger when someone sins against us. This is why Paul wrote:

> *"Be angry, and yet do not sin; do not let the sun go down on your anger..."*

> Ephesians 4:26

The phrase "be angry" is written as an imperative—that is, a command. God is saying, "I command you to be angry, but not for very long. Do not let the sun go down on your anger." There is right reason for us to be angry. We should be angry at the same things that make God angry—sin. We should feel angry at sins, but not for very long. We need to practice Personal Forgiveness right away so that our anger is replaced with God's love.

The best time to forgive someone is actually when you are feeling the angriest at them. Just like receiving God's forgiveness, forgiving others with our head alone will make our forgiveness shallow.

We need to talk with God about our pain and anger regarding this sin. When we believe that God is feeling the same pain we do, we feel His comfort. When we believe that God is intensely angry at the same sin we are, we feel His validation. And as I said in our discussion of the first path of forgiveness, sometimes our emotions can be so overwhelming that we need other people as well. God can comfort and validate us through other people as they share in our pain and anger.

We need to feel what God feels together with Him—the pain of and anger at sin.

Step 3. ACKNOWLEDGE God's just penalty for this sin—condemn what God condemns

It is helpful to ask ourselves out loud, "If Jesus had not come, what would a holy and just God have to do to this person who sinned against me in order to bring about divine justice?" Then say the biblical answer out loud, "God would have to execute him." Now examine yourself—how do you feel about this? With some sins, this may feel entirely appropriate. However, with other sins and the sins of people you love, you may struggle with this. I sure did. After several years of teaching others the divine penalty for sins, one night I came to a crisis of belief.

> **The best time to forgive is when we are feeling the angriest.**

I came home late one evening from a church meeting. As I walked to the front door by the big front window, I noticed something strange. All six of our children were still up. All of them were in the family room doing a variety of things. Michael, our oldest (at the time he was 18), was playing a computer game. To my dismay, I saw my expensive new guitar, which I had received as a gift, lying in the middle of the floor, only partially in its case, with the lid wide open. Some of our youngest children were running around the room. All I could imagine was one of them falling onto the guitar and destroying it. I was instantly angry, and I knew who was responsible, Michael. At the time, Michael was the only other person in our house who played guitar, but he did not have permission to use this guitar.

So I exercised self-control (not forgiveness), suppressing my anger as I came into the room. I then said firmly, "Who left my guitar lying so vulnerably in the middle of the room?" I wanted to give Michael the best opportunity to respond in a loving and repentant way.

Without pausing or looking up, Michael said, "I did, Dad."

The way he responded made me angrier. I then said, "I want you to get up right now and put it away properly before it gets damaged."

Still typing away on his computer, with a deep sigh of irritation, Michael said, "In a moment."

My anger flared up even more, and I said with a louder voice, "No. I want you to get up right now and take care of this. You didn't even have permission to use it."

Now Michael was upset with me for interrupting his game. Giving another deep sigh, he got up and quickly started shoving the guitar into its case so he could get back to his game. But he wasn't doing it carefully—he was sure to damage the guitar with his carelessness. My anger shot up higher. I grabbed the guitar away from him and put it in the case myself.

By now all the other children had scattered, like cockroaches when the light is turned on. They knew Michael was in trouble and thought it best to get to bed. Becky had turned from her computer to watch like a referee, in case I committed a 'foul' against Michael, or he against me.

Realizing that I was overwhelmed with anger, and not wanting to act out, I quickly decided to remove myself from the situation to practice forgiveness. I told Becky and Michael that I needed to go out and process what had happened. So I got in my car, started down a dark country road near my house and began working through the six basic steps of Personal Forgiveness.

First, I needed to identify the sin. Anger always indicates that someone has sinned or is sinning.[22] Following Jesus' instructions, I looked for the log in my own eye first. I asked God, "Lord, am I angry at Michael because I am sinning against him in some way? Do I love this new guitar more than I love Michael?" As I thought about this and listened, I didn't discover any sin on my part.

So I asked God, "Has Michael sinned against me in some way?" And immediately a command came to mind: "You shall honor your father and mother." This is one of the Ten Commandments, a law built on love. Then I thought, "Jesus wouldn't use his father's guitar without first asking to do so. Nor would he neglect it by leaving it in an open guitar case, on the floor, in the middle of a room full of energetic children. Nor would he fail to get up and take care of the problem immediately when the situation was pointed out to him. Nor would he sigh like that, communicating that his dad was an irritant to him."

Very quickly I had identified some of Michael's sins against me. Then

I realized that he had been disrespecting me in these same ways for months. I'd felt it before, but I thought that if I just ignored it I would be okay and Michael's behavior would change for the better by itself. I felt hurt and sad that my own son, whom I love and into whom I had poured so much of my time, energy and life, didn't really care about me or what was important to me. Identifying this sin made me even angrier than I was at home! I talked with God about this for a while. I thought about how my sins make Him feel the same way I was feeling. I was guilty of some of the same sins as Michael. I confessed them to God and received His forgiveness. Then I went back to work on Michael's sins against me.

I had identified some of Michael's sins and knew that he was responsible for them. I was experiencing the hurt and the anger triggered by these sins and had talked with God about our shared emotions. Now I needed to move on to step three—condemn what God condemns. So I asked myself out loud, "If Jesus had not come, what would a holy and just God have to do to Michael in order to bring about divine justice in light of these sins?" I then said out loud, "God would have to execute him."

But as soon as I said this, something happened inside me. All my anger towards Michael immediately disappeared—not because I had forgiven Michael, but because my parental instincts kicked in. I wanted to protect my son! I didn't like the idea that God would execute my child. Without even thinking, I blurted out loud to God, "No, God, not my son!"

The next thought in my head surprised me, because it was something I would never have thought on my own. I heard a firm voice saying, "Get out of my way. Your son sinned against Me." I had to think about that for some time. You see, I had been thinking about Michael's sin only as a sin against me. God was reminding me that all sins are first and foremost

---

22 Often times our anger is because someone has in fact sinned against us. However, sometimes we can feel angry at someone not because of their sins, but because of our sins. When we **expect** people to do what we want them to do, the way we want them to do it, when we want them to do it, we feel angry if they do not meet our expectations. For example, when a wife does have sex with her husband when he wants it, the way he wants it, he may get angry, not necessarily because she is sinning, but because she is not living up to his expectations. Sometimes we feel anger out of proportion to the sin committed because that sin was similar to a sin committed against us in the past that has not yet been dealt with and healed.

against Him. Michael had sinned against God when he disrespected me. As I drove on, this truth sank deeper into my soul, and God kept silent for several minutes.

Then I heard God say, "By the way, Michael is My son, not yours." (I knew that this was also from God because I would never have thought of saying that). I was trying to protect Michael from God, standing between them, because I wrongly believed that I had more responsibility for Michael than God did. What a ridiculous way of thinking! I am Michael's physical, earthly father. God is Michael's eternal, Heavenly Father. I needed to change my thinking about how God and I were related to Michael.

God said one more thing to me—something that embarrassed me. I heard in my thoughts, "And I never sin against Michael." God was reminding me that He never sins. I, however, had sinned against Michael countless times. God was saying, "Steve, if you think you love Michael more than I do, then think again! You sin against him. I do not. I love Michael far, far more than you do. Don't even begin to think that you are more righteous or more loving than Me, or that you need to protect Michael from Me. I will always do what is good and right and loving and just. Get out of my way. Your son sinned against Me."

It took another 20 minutes of driving and remembering Bible verses (many of which I have shared with you in this book) before I could finally change my mind and agree with God's holy, just and divine penalty for Michael's sin. God showed me that night that I didn't yet really believe what I was teaching. I didn't really believe that *any* and every sin deserves physical execution by God. God changed me that night. I haven't had a problem with this step since then. God may need to bring you through a similar experience to deepen your own conviction of this truth, but it will only happen as you practice forgiveness. I share this with you in advance, so you won't be surprised when it happens.

We will not be able to believe that Jesus died to pay the penalty for anyone's sin if we do not first believe that the penalty for that sin is physical execution by God. However, when we do believe it, we are ready for the next step.

Step 4. EMBRACE THE EXECUTION OF JESUS as the full and just payment for this sin—accept what God accepts

Now we need to ask this question—"Is God going to execute the person who has sinned against me?" The biblical answer is "no." Why not? Because Jesus Christ has already been executed in that person's place for that particular sin. God has already sent away that person's need to pay the penalty for that sin. When we forgive people, we are not really doing anything. Rather, we are discovering that God has already forgiven them at the cross. We are simply joining God in something He has already done. We are accepting what He has already accepted.

When we don't embrace Jesus' death as the full and just payment for someone's sin as God has, we are saying that Jesus' work on the cross is insufficient.

This is why withholding forgiveness is an incredible insult to God. It is itself a sin with terrible consequences. The more we can see and feel the reality of what Jesus has accomplished on the cross, however, the more driven we are to want to enter into God's forgiveness of those who sin against us—even our enemies! We will see forgiving others as a gift from God and will want to thank Him for it.

Step 5. COMMUNICATE with the appropriate person—God

What does the person who sinned against us need to do for us to forgive them? Absolutely nothing. *We don't even need to tell them that we are forgiving them in order to forgive them.* Forgiving someone of the penalty for their sin is unconditional and has nothing to do with the guilty person at all. This means that we can forgive dead people, unrepentant people, non-Christians, anyone and everyone. Remember what Jesus said in Mark 11:25,

> *Whenever you stand praying, if you have anything against anyone, forgive...*

Personal Forgiveness is something that happens between us and God. So when we are forgiving someone who has sinned against us, the person we need to talk to is God. Again, this prayer simply follows the pattern of the six basic steps of Personal Forgiveness. We should:

- *Identify the sin and the person responsible for it*
- *Talk with God about how we feel and how He feels about this sin*
- *Agree with God's just condemnation of this sin*
- *Thank Jesus for paying for this sin*
- *Thank God for forgiving this person of the penalty for this sin*
- *Tell God that we are joining Him in His forgiveness of this sin*
- *Ask God to show us how to love this person appropriately with the love God has for them*

The prayer might sound like this.

> *Heavenly Father, thank you for showing me how Michael sinned against You and victimized me when he did not respect me as his dad. Thank You for feeling my pain, and for being even angrier at this sin than I am. I accept the truth that even though you love Michael, if not for Jesus, You would have to execute him because You are holy and just. However, I know that you are not going to punish Michael, because You already executed Jesus in his place for this sin. Thank you, Jesus, for dying for Michael. Thank you, God, for forgiving Michael of the penalty for this sin. I agree with and join in Your forgiveness of Michael. Now, Lord, please show me how to love Michael appropriately with the love You have for him. Amen.*

As I prayed this prayer that night, I could feel God's love for Michael. I could feel Jesus dying for Michael. I could feel God's forgiveness of Michael—and I joined Him in it. No longer was my anger just suppressed by parental love. It was removed and replaced with God's love. I will tell you the rest of the story in the next chapter.

Step 6. Let God's LOVE flow—love as God loves

Anger is the emotional experience of this thought—"You hurt me and I need to see you suffer!"

Personal Forgiveness is the exact opposite. It is the emotional experience of this thought—

> *You hurt me by sinning against God. He should have executed you, but because Jesus has died in your place for this sin, I don't need to see you suffer. My heart's cry for justice has been satisfied at the cross. I now want to see God bless you and, if appropriate, I want to be a part of that blessing!*

Real forgiveness not only removes our anger—it actually replaces our anger with God's love. A good indication that real forgiveness has taken place is a growing love for the offender. This truly is a miracle from God. Because of His gift of forgiveness, we can love our enemies the same way God does.

Several years ago, Becky and I were on a ministry trip in Honduras, Central America. We were in a small town on the Atlantic coast called Tela Mar. I will never forget the last day we were there. It was a Sunday, November 1. On that day I was robbed of my wedding ring.

> **Learn to thank Jesus for dying for the people who have sinned against you.**

On this particular morning I was walking along the inland side of the beach, close to the jungle. It was so hot I was wearing just my swim shorts. As I approached the town, I passed the cemetery. Since it was the Day of the Dead, many people were bringing food, alcohol and cigarettes to the cemetery to honor their deceased relatives. As I stood and watched for a moment, my heart went out to these people. Most of them would consider themselves Christians, but they were still trapped in untrue and unhelpful ways of thinking about Jesus. So I prayed for a while asking God to help these people to see the light and the love of Jesus. I then continued on back to the house where we were staying.

As I walked down the path, I saw a young man sitting under a tree, smoking a cigarette. When I got closer he threw his cigarette down, jumped up, grabbed his machete and ran up to me, waving his machete and yelling at me in Spanish. He was pointing at my watch. I didn't speak very much Spanish, but I was fairly sure that he wanted to rob me.

Almost immediately I realized that God was answering my prayer. God wanted me to show him the light and the love of Jesus. I knew that Jesus had died for all of this man's sins, including the sin of threatening and robbing me. I forgave him immediately. So I wasn't angry at him—instead, I wanted to bless him with the love of God. I wanted to be like Jesus to him. I asked myself, "How would Jesus respond to this man?"

I gave my watch to him. It was rather easy to give him a digital watch worth about $10. I also gave him my New Testament. He found the 100-limpera bill (worth about $7.50 US) in it that I was using as a bookmark. Taking the bill, he gave the book back to me, but I forced it back into his hands and said, "If you are going to rob me you will have the take the Bible, too." He quickly reached around my hip and patted my left buttocks, disappointed to find that I didn't have a wallet with me.

At that point I assumed that I had given him all I had on me, hoping he didn't want my swimming trunks. He pointed at my left hand. I looked around, thinking he was pointing at something behind me. Then I realized he wanted my wedding ring. This

> "Real forgiveness leads to real love."

was going to be very difficult to give over. I tried to get it off, but my knuckles were so swollen from my hike and the heat that I couldn't get it off. When I showed him my difficulty, he motioned as if he might cut my finger off to get the ring. So I tried a little harder.

While I worked on getting my ring off, I started talking with him, speaking in the little, broken Spanish I knew. (I prayed to speak in tongues. I suggested Spanish, but nothing came). He was wearing a cross, so I asked him how he could wear a cross and rob people. He didn't understand. When I finally removed my wedding ring and put it in his hand, I knew there was nothing more I could give him. I asked God what I should do next. I thought, "Pray."

I looked at my friend (I was calling him "amigo," Spanish for "friend" every time I could), pressed my hands together and said, "I am going to pray for you." Then I knelt down in the sand in front of him and started to pray out loud in English. I prayed for my friend. I prayed for his family.

I prayed for the town, their poverty and the spiritual darkness they lived in. I even started crying for them. I prayed for at least 10 minutes. Then I said, "Amen."

To my amazement, I heard my "amigo" say, "Amen." I looked up and there he was, kneeling in the sand in front of me, with his head bowed. The machete was stuck in the sand behind him. He had been praying with me, even though he didn't speak English. (Perhaps he heard my prayer in Spanish). I was astonished. I sat down in front of him to see what would happen next. He sat down with me, lit up a cigarette and started telling me about his life... in Spanish. I understood very little of it, except that both his parents were buried in the cemetery behind me. He talked for about 10 minutes.

I then told him I was a pastor, and that the book I had given him was a Bible. He understood these things. At that point I remembered that I had a Spanish-English New Testament back at the house where we were staying. I told him that if he waited for me, I would bring him a Spanish Bible. He understood and agreed, so I stood up. He remained seated. If I wanted to get my ring back, I now had positional advantage—I am 6 feet, 3 inches tall and he was only about 5 feet 5 inches tall, underweight from malnourishment, and his weapon was stuck in the sand behind him. It would have been easy to get my ring back, but I didn't think that was what Jesus would do. I heard God say to me, "You can have your ring, or you can have this man's soul. Make your choice." So I shook his hand with a smile and started to walk back to the house.

I hurried back to our room and found the Spanish-English New Testament. I put another 100-limpera bill as a bookmark at Matthew 5:38-41 where Jesus says, "You have heard it said, 'An eye for an eye and a tooth for a tooth,' but I say to you, do not resist an evil person; but whoever slaps you on the right cheek, turn to him the other also. If anyone wants to sue you and take your shirt, give him your coat also. Whoever forces you to go one mile, go with him two." I then ran back to the tree where I had been robbed.

Unfortunately, he was gone. I suppose he just couldn't believe that anyone he had just robbed would come back without the police. Again I prayed for my new friend, for his family and for his town. I knew that what Satan had meant for evil, God meant for good.[24] I then left the

24 Genesis 50:20

132

New Testament with its bookmark in the tree, hoping he would return and find it later.

This man, my "amigo," is the only person in Honduras that I regularly pray for. I don't know who he is or where he is, but God knows. I continue to love him the only way I can, by praying for him. This is God's love, not mine. If I hadn't forgiven him while he was sinning against me, who knows what would have happened. Perhaps we would have gotten into a fight. One of us could possibly have lost a hand, an arm or our life. Or I might be living in anger and resentment to this day over a sin someone committed against me decades ago. He might still be living in darkness, not having experienced, in a very personal way, the light and the love of Jesus. Real forgiveness leads to real love.

After forgiving someone of the penalty for their sins, we need to pray and find out how God wants us to love that person with His love in appropriate ways. The key word here is "appropriate." Love doesn't mean that we should trust the people who sin against us, be friends with them, marry them, lend money to them, go into business with them, etc. The people we forgive are still the same people who sinned against us, unless they repent. We are to love all people just as God loves them, but love can take many different shapes and forms. *How we love repentant people is very different from how we love unrepentant* people. It is also true that how we are to love family members is different from how we are to love strangers, coworkers or neighbors. How we are to love men is different from how we are to love women. Discovering how to love different people, guilty of different sins, at different times, takes prayer, practice and time. God, the Author of Love Himself, will help us.

Third Path of Forgiveness—Asking People to Forgive Us of the Penalty for Our Sins

Unlike the first two paths of Personal Forgiveness, asking someone to forgive us involves talking with another human being. We do not need to ask God to forgive us of the penalty for our sins because He already has. However, most people we have sinned against have not yet forgiven us. We need to go to them, taking responsibility for what we have done, feeling the reality of our sin, and ask them to forgive us. We need to ask in a way that gives them the best opportunity to actually forgive us so that God can heal them. Practicing the first two paths of Personal Forgiveness will help prepare your heart, your mind and your words for this path.

Step 1. IDENTIFY your sins against another person— see what God sees

While looking for sins in one path, it is common to find sins in the other two paths as well. So by the time you get through the first two paths of Personal Forgiveness, you may already have identified some sins you have committed against others.

Or perhaps someone is angry at you, disappointed in you, frustrated with you or tired of you. When people feel this way about us, we need to pray, asking God to show us if we have sinned against them. It is, however, very important to remember that someone's negative feelings don't guarantee that we have sinned against them—they may instead indicate that they are sinning against us. Jesus did everything right, but that made some people very mad at Him. It is important to listen to what others have to say about us, but we must always be careful to listen to what God says through His Word and His Son, more so than others' opinions.

Nevertheless, as Jesus said, it is always prudent to look first for our own sins before looking for other people's sins.

Why do you look at the speck that is in your brother's eye, but do not notice the log that is in your own eye? Or how can you say to your brother, "Let me take the speck out of your eye," and behold, the log is in your own eye? You hypocrite, first take the log out of your own eye, and then you will see clearly to take the speck out of your brother's eye.

Matthew 7:3-5

We can have a difficult time seeing our own sins against people because we are blinded by their sins against us and our anger towards them. Even when we feel we are much less at fault than they are, we must be responsible for our sin and deal with it appropriately. We will see our sins much more clearly and easily after forgiving the other person. This is why we need to forgive them before we work on asking them to forgive us.

When looking for your sins against others, it might be very helpful to compare your thoughts, words and actions with what Jesus might have done in your place. Ask God, "How have I not loved my parent/spouse/sibling/boss/teachers/neighbors the way Jesus would have loved them in my place?"

Again, this is only going to be helpful if you know Jesus truly from God's Word.

Now, if you find a sin you haven't yet confessed to God, go back and practice the first path of Personal Forgiveness before you move on in this third path. If we don't receive God's forgiveness before asking others to forgive us, we will be asking a human being to give us an experience of forgiveness that only God can give us. We will end up asking *for forgiveness* rather than asking people *to forgive us*.

Asking people *to forgive* us is an act of love because it focuses on helping the person we have hurt receive God's healing by forgiving us. Asking *for forgiveness* is focused on self—I need healing, *I'm hurting, I* want this to stop... Asking others *for forgiveness* can be done in a very needy, hurtful and sinful way. We need to make sure that we first receive what we

> **We don't need to ask God to forgive us because He already has. We do need to ask people to forgive us because most likely they have not.**

need from God so we can help others receive what they need from God. We try to give them the best opportunity to do that by confessing our sin and sincerely, appropriately asking them *to* forgive us.

Step 2. FEEL the reality of the sin together with God— feel what they feel

Before we ask people to forgive us, we need to feel, as best we can, the pain we have caused them. Asking people to forgive us without feeling their pain will appear insincere and callous. As with God, the best time to confess a sin to others is when we are feeling the most sorrow and regret for what we have done to them. God feels their pain. He will help us feel it, too, when we ask Him.

God feels their anger, too. We need to listen to God and accept their anger towards us as their heart's cry for justice. *Now I don't mean that we should accept their sinful expressions of anger.* It is one thing to feel angry—it is quite another to act out in anger and hurt people. If someone is hurting you in anger, then that person is sinning against you, even if you sinned against them first. In those cases you will need to set up God-authorized boundaries and forgive them before you can ask them to forgive you. We will talk about boundaries in the next chapter.

> **The best time to ask someone to forgive you is when you are feeling the most sorrow for the pain you have caused them.**

Step 3. Acknowledge God's just penalty for this sin— CONDEMN what God condemns

While preparing ourselves to ask others to forgive us, it will help us to remember the severity of the penalty of our sin against them, even though we would have already done this while working through the first path of forgiveness.

We must also consider what we might need to say to the person we have sinned against. Do they know Jesus? Do they understand the cross? Are they familiar with the divine penalty for sins? What is their definition of forgiveness? What will they think we are asking for when we ask them to forgive us? Depending on the person, when asking them to forgive you, you may need to briefly include what you mean by forgiveness. I will show you what this might sound like when we get to step 5.

Step 4. EMBRACE THE EXECUTION OF JESUS as the full and just payment for this sin—accept what God accepts

This step, too, is something we would already have done with God. However, many people do not understand biblical forgiveness. They think forgiveness means minimizing, excusing, justifying, pretending the sin didn't happen, etc. When we ask them to forgive us, they will most likely think we are asking them to forgive us according to their definition of forgiveness—or their coping mechanism. This can be a grave mistake. So again, depending on the person, you may need to briefly explain what real forgiveness is as you ask them to forgive you.

Step 5. COMMUNICATE with the appropriate person— to the person you sinned against

Asking someone to forgive us can be challenging. Once we have prepared ourselves to make this request, we need to prepare our words. It is far too easy to say the wrong things, or to say the right things in the wrong way. It is much wiser to prepare our words beforehand—even to the extent of writing them out—and to practice our well thought-out words exactly as we would say them when making our request.

Here are some basic guidelines:

- *Be specific.* What sin are you confessing?

- *Be empathetic.* People need to see that you feel what you've done to them.

- *Be repentant.* If it isn't clear that you have stopped doing this sin already, the person is going to want to know if you are going to continue hurting them. If you stole something, are you going to return it? Are you willing to accept the consequences of your sin without complaint?

- *Be clear.* You are confessing a sin and taking responsibility for a wrong that you have done. You are asking this person to forgive you so that they will be healed. Most of the time, you will need to explain what you are asking this person to do.

- *Be brief.* Too many words will confuse your listener.

- *Be sincere:* People will quickly sense if you are insincere, acting or pretending, and will be reluctant to believe you. That's why it is so important to prepare your heart before you ask for forgiveness, humbly and honestly.

- *Be yourself.* Your words might sound something like what I've written below, but you will need to modify them, or at least practice them, to make them your own.

  > *"God has convicted me that I sinned against you by (name the sin). When I did this, I wasn't loving you the way God loves you. I may never fully feel the pain I caused you, but I know that I hurt you and I deeply regret it. God hates what I did to you. And though I don't deserve it, Jesus Christ died to pay the penalty for what I did to you. Would you please believe that Jesus has fully paid for my sin, and would you please forgive me?"*

Once you have prepared your words, ask God to help you set up the appropriate time and place to make your request. It is normally best to make confession and ask for forgiveness in person. Using the phone or mail can just be another way of hiding. However, there are exceptions. For instance, it would be inappropriate for a rapist to try and make an appointment with his victim, or even to call her. In such cases, it might be necessary to write a letter. If you don't know where the person lives, ask God. If the person is dead, I would recommend talking to an appropriate family member of theirs.

Be careful of asking someone to forgive you the next time you see them. Avoid asking for forgiveness just in passing, as if it were something of little significance. Confessing sins is important enough to warrant making an appointment—even if it may only be pulling someone aside in a timely fashion for a quick private conversation. For more serious sins, however, it may mean making a phone call to set a meeting someplace quiet and safe for both of you.

Sometimes you will be asking someone who is unrepentant, intimidating or dangerous to be with in person. **Use common sense in these cases.** If necessary, bring someone with you and/or do it in public, to reduce the possibility of being victimized again. Be very careful about writing a letter. Experience has shown that we should avoid asking someone to forgive us by mail, and definitely not by texting on a phone. Written forms of communication are often misconstrued and can quickly spark more sins.

Use the words you prepared and practiced. Tension and unexpected interruptions can result in spontaneous speech, which often backfires and makes matters worse.

When we ask people to forgive us, sometimes they may give us an immediate answer, but other times people will ask for more information. They may ask what we mean by forgiveness. They may test us to see if we really feel the pain we have caused them. They may want to measure our level of repentance, or hear our plans for restitution (if appropriate, as in the case of stealing). They may start confessing their own sins to us. There may be interruptions. All kinds of things can happen. Of course, they may just want more time to think about it.

Whatever happens, you will need to deal with their questions honestly and briefly. Ultimately, it will be good for them to *give us a response.*

We may need to be quiet for a while and let them think. Be patient. Remember, we are trying to help them to forgive us so that God can heal them. If they want more time, give them more time. Just be sure to follow up on your request later.

You also need to be prepared for a variety of responses. No matter how they respond, you must be prepared to respond lovingly and graciously.

If they say "yes," of course you will want to thank them.

If they say "no," it *might* be appropriate to ask why they feel that they cannot forgive you presently. Perhaps they don't understand forgiveness. Perhaps they don't realize that you are willing to suffer the consequences of your sin without complaint. Perhaps they don't sense sincerity or empathy. Perhaps there are other sins, more serious sins you have overlooked.

> **People will not necessarily forgive you, even when you ask them to in the best possible way.**

However, it isn't always appropriate to ask why someone doesn't want to forgive you. Remember, you don't need this person to forgive you for your sake. People need to forgive you **for their own sake**. Your confession and request is a way of giving them the opportunity to do this. Of course, if this is a relationship that could and should have flourished when recovered, then it will be a loss for both of you if this person never forgives you. For this, you can truly grieve.

Regardless of how this person responds, God will deepen your healing when you practice this path of Personal Forgiveness with sincerity and empathy.

Step 6. Let God's LOVE flow—love as God loves

Taking responsibility for our actions, confessing our sins to the people we have harmed and asking them to forgive us is just the beginning of loving the people we have sinned against. Next, we need to discover how God wants us to appropriately expand and deepen our loving actions towards them. Again, love takes many shapes and forms—depending on gender, the kind of relationship, social customs, the kind and frequency of past sins, how much damage those sins have caused and more. We need to be prudent and prayerful. And we need to remember that love means doing what is best for the other person, not for us. Sometimes the only way to appropriately love someone we have sinned against is through prayer. However, usually there is much, much more we can do to love them with the love God has for them.

Additional Steps in Personal Forgiveness

In addition to the six basic steps of Personal Forgiveness, there are other steps that, although not necessary for practicing forgiveness, can magnify and deepen its benefits.

For example, when God heals us and sets us free from years of hurt and dysfunction, our new freedom is worth celebrating! Also, evicting demonic influences is not necessary to practice forgiveness, but the best time to evict demons is when we practice forgiveness. In addition, sharing your story of forgiveness with others when it is appropriate will help them and will also deepen your experience of forgiveness.[25]

What's Next?

Through Personal Forgiveness and its three paths, God heals and transforms the human soul. However, this is just one half of biblical forgiveness. There's more. God also heals and transforms relationships through our practice of the other half of biblical forgiveness—Relational Forgiveness. We can now move on to its six principles.

---

25 If you would like to know more about these additional steps you will find them in our study book, "Developing a Lifestyle of Forgiveness," which is designed for individuals and small groups.

SUMMARY

- There are six basics steps to practice Personal Forgiveness well:

  Step 1. IDENTIFY the sin and the person(s) responsible for it—see what God sees

  Step 2: **FEEL** the reality of the sin together with God—feel what God feels

  Step 3. Acknowledge God's just penalty for this sin—**CONDEMN** what God condemns

  Step 4. EMBRACE THE EXECUTION OF JESUS as the full and just payment for this sin—accept what God accepts

  Step 5. COMMUNICATE with the appropriate person—speak to the person God would have you speak with

  Step 6. Let God's **LOVE** flow—love as God loves

- Love is the fruit of real forgiveness

- Each path of Personal Forgiveness brings healing to prepare us for the next path

- We need to practice the three paths of forgiveness in proper order:
  1. First path first - Receive God's forgiveness
  2. Second path second - Forgive others
  3. Third path third - Ask others to forgive us

CHAPTER SIX

How to Practice Relational Forgiveness

The Sixth Key Concept of Forgiveness

There are six principles to the practice of Relational Forgiveness

Not all consequences of sin are relational in nature, but many of them negatively affect our relationships with God and with others. Relational Forgiveness is the forgiveness of these consequences, conditional on the guilty person's repentance. Since the ultimate goal of God's forgiveness is to establish loving relationships, it makes sense to call this side of forgiveness *Relational Forgiveness*.

> Relational Forgiveness is reducing the negative consequences of a sin appropriate to the guilty person's level of repentance.

God wants to have a personal, loving relationship with each and every person. He has already forgiven everyone of the penalty for their sins through the cross, but this doesn't mean that He has a loving relationship with any of them. A relationship isn't a *loving relationship* if only one person loves. In a loving relationship, *both* persons love each other. God loves people unconditionally and perfectly. For this reason *He is giving people the best opportunities* to repent so they can love Him and enter a loving relationship with Him.

God also wants us to have personal, loving relationships with one another. We are to always love all people whether they love us or not. However, you can only have a loving relationship with people who also love you. So we need to follow God's pattern in *giving the people who sin against us the very best opportunities* to repent and enter a loving relationship with us. To do this, we need to learn the six principles of Relational Forgiveness.

God established these principles and is following them Himself as He extends Relational Forgiveness to us. As with Personal Forgiveness, the principles are the same for all three paths of forgiveness. This means understanding these principles will:

1. Teach us how to cooperate with God so that He can forgive the consequences of our sins,

2. Enable us to practice Relational Forgiveness towards those who have sinned against us and

3. Teach us how best to respond to the people we have sinned against, so they might forgive the consequences of our sins against them.

They are called *principles* rather than steps because they are more like general guidelines than fixed steps. These principles are practiced differently with each unique person and in each unique situation. Practicing Relational Forgiveness requires flexibility, thought, imagination, listening and learning. It involves trial and error and learning from our mistakes. It is also often assisted by the wise counsel of other people.

> "There is no one right way to practice Relational Forgiveness in every situation. "

Relational Forgiveness also involves a lot of conversation with God in prayer. God knows the way to give someone the best opportunity to repent. We do not. We need to ask Him for specific directions and His empowerment to carry them out. In this way, Relational Forgiveness is like a journey, and the six principles like a compass, pointing us in the right direction.

These are the principles:

- **First Principle.** Practice all three paths of *PERSONAL FORGIVENESS FIRST*

- **Second Principle.** Let the guilty person's level of *REPENTANCE* guide the process

- **Third Principle.** Let *REAL CHANGE* verify authentic repentance

- **Fourth Principle.** Follow through with appropriate *CONSEQUENCES*

- **Fifth Principle.** Establish God-authorized *BOUNDARIES*

- **Sixth Principle.** Evaluate the progress and *ADJUST* the consequences and boundaries as appropriate

As with the steps of Personal Forgiveness, I have highlighted the key words or phrases to help you remember them. Now let's begin by examining each principle.

First Principle. Practice all three paths of PERSONAL FORGIVENESS FIRST

Without practicing Personal Forgiveness, we remain bound up in guilt, shame, fear, hurt, anger, depression, etc. Our soul remains damaged and dysfunctional. We are unable to love like God loves. **We will be unable to practice Relational Forgiveness well.** However, when we practice Personal Forgiveness, God heals us, frees us, empowers us and motivates us. We see more clearly without the blinding and disabling effects of sin. We find ourselves increasingly filled with God's love and able to do what we would never have been able to before. *Always, always practice all three paths of Personal Forgiveness first.*

Second Principle. Let the guilty person's level of REPENTANCE guide the process

> *"As I live!" declares the Lord God, "I take no pleasure in the death of the wicked, but rather that the wicked turn from his way and live."*
>
> Ezekiel 33:11

God wants to heal and restore loving relationships, but He cannot do it when people want to continue in sin. This second principle is simply built upon this basic truth. Repentance of a sin must always come before the consequences can be forgiven.

So we must be attentive to a person's *level* of repentance. People are rarely completely repentant or completely unrepentant. Recall your own experiences of resisting certain sins. On some days you may find it very easy to resist it, but on other days, much less so. What we need to see in ourselves and others is a *movement towards deeper and deeper levels of repentance.* Is there a growing awareness of how much damage and pain the sin causes? Is there a growing hatred of the sin? Are there stronger efforts to eliminate the root causes of the sin? There is no machine that can measure repentance—we must watch and pray and learn.

Third Principle. LET REAL CHANGE verify authentic repentance

No one can stop committing a sin until they first want to stop committing that sin. Real repentance must start in the heart and mind before moving out into action. God can see into the heart and intent, and can act as soon as He sees a change of mind. We, however, cannot read minds and must wait until we see a change in behavior. That's what this principle is about. *Real repentance always results in a change of behavior.*

Truly repentant people will always try to do something different. It may or may not work, but they will always do **something** to try and change their behavior. That's why John the Baptist said to the Pharisees and Sadducees who came to be baptized by him,

> *You brood of vipers, who warned you to flee from the wrath*
> *to come? Therefore bear fruit in keeping with repentance.*
> Matthew 3:7-8

John was not willing to treat them as repentant people until they first demonstrated in some **visible way** that they were truly repentant.

How will you know if you are truly repentant of a sin? You will know when you see yourself doing something different to change. The same goes for knowing if someone else is truly repentant.

We don't have the **power** or the **understanding** to effect real change in ourselves. We will never overcome sin in our lives by our own efforts or our sheer willpower. We need God to empower us and show us what we need to do differently for Him to change us from the inside out. This is why true repentance involves crying out to God for help and then following His directions. Making promises "never to do it again" to God, to others or to yourself will not work to truly change us. We must learn to depend on God and follow His directions.

Fourth Principle. Follow through with appropriate CONSEQUENCES

God designed a world of order, of cause and effect, of actions and consequences. This is why Paul wrote,

> *Do not be deceived, God is not mocked; for whatever a man sows, this he will also reap. For the one who sows to his own flesh will from the flesh reap corruption, but the one who sows to the Spirit will from the Spirit reap eternal life.*
>
> Galatians 6:7-8

God always follows through with appropriate consequences for everything people think, do and say. Our thoughts, words and deeds are like seeds. Either we are planting the seeds of love by the Spirit which reap the consequences of "life," or we are planting the seeds of sin which reap the consequences of "corruption." When God follows through with the negative consequences of sin, it isn't because He doesn't love the sinner. Rather it is because He does love the sinner.

> *I now rejoice, not that you were made sorrowful, but that you were made sorrowful to the point of repentance; for you were made sorrowful according to the will of God, so that you might not suffer loss in anything through us. For the sorrow that is according to the will of God produces a repentance without regret, leading to salvation, but the sorrow of the world produces death.*
>
> 2 Corinthians 7:9-10

When we are unrepentant, God administers the painful consequences of sin for the purpose of *motivating us to stop sinning*—to stop destroying our lives and the lives of people around us. When we do repent of our sin, then God will also follow through with the positive consequences of repentance. Thus, when people sin against us, we also must carefully and lovingly administer appropriate consequences, in order to help motivate them to repent. And when they repent, we must change those consequences to match their level of repentance.

> **The purpose of administering the painful consequences of sin is to motivate people to stop sinning.**

I have repeated and emphasized the word "appropriate" in the past few paragraphs because it is so important—because human beings often want to follow through with inappropriate consequences. Consequences can be used as a form of revenge, and a weapon to hurt someone, to punish them, to get even.

If we find ourselves inflicting consequences that are too severe for the sin or the guilty person, then we need to examine ourselves. Perhaps we haven't really forgiven this person of the penalty for their sin. Or perhaps we haven't yet forgiven them deeply enough. Or perhaps this person has committed other sins against us that we haven't forgiven at all. Or perhaps we are angry at someone else who has sinned against us, and lashing out at the wrong person. When people don't practice Personal Forgiveness adequately, they are likely to overreact when applying consequences.

Remember, God's anger has been satisfied, and the penalty for sin has been paid, at the cross, once for all by Jesus. God does not use consequences to punish people. He uses consequences as a ministry for their good, to move them towards repentance. So we also must be careful to ensure we are using consequences in a loving manner for the good of those who have sinned against us.

Sometimes people may underreact and apply consequences that aren't strong enough. They think that letting a sin slide by with zero or minimal consequences is the *loving* thing to do. It isn't. People need to feel the painful consequences of their sin. Otherwise, they would think they can continue in sin and get away with it. Allowing this is harmful, not helpful or loving, to them. God does not do this, and neither should we.

Discovering the appropriate consequences for a particular sin committed by a particular person requires prayer, discernment and wisdom.

When God administers appropriate consequences, He sometimes uses what we may call natural consequences. We call them "natural" because they flow logically out of the order of the world. When we put our hand on a hot stove, we get burned. When we don't eat properly, we become weak or get sick. Natural consequences also happen in relationships. People are less likely to trust someone who lies. A thief will probably be fired from his workplace.

God may also use human agents—like governments—to administer appropriate consequences for sin.

> *For rulers are not a cause of fear for good behavior, but for evil.*
> *Do you want to have no fear of authority? Do what is good and*
> *you will have praise from the same; for it is a minister of God*
> *to you for good. But if you do what is evil, be afraid; for it does*
> *not bear the sword for nothing; for it is a minister of God, an*
> *avenger who brings wrath on the one who practices evil.*
>
> Romans 13:3-4

Human governments serve to restrain many sins by enforcing laws and administering painful consequences. But this is not to say that all human governments and laws lovingly and uprightly administer appropriate consequences. Governments are comprised of sinful people who often use civil power as an opportunity to selfishly take advantage of other people. But God does use governments to administer appropriate consequences.

Other human agents include parents (who administer appropriate consequences for the sake of their children), spouses (who administer consequences to one another), employers (to employees) and church members (to one another). In fact, most consequences aren't administered formally. They happen automatically in our everyday relationships.

The important truth to remember about this principle is its purpose. The purpose of administering the appropriate negative consequences for a sin is to **motivate the guilty person to repent.**

However, this brings us to another important truth. Negative consequences do not always work in bringing about repentance. Sometimes people insist on doing what they want to do, no matter how much it hurts. In the Bible, this is called being hardhearted or stiff-necked.

> *A man who hardens his neck after much reproof will*
> *suddenly be broken beyond remedy.*
>
> Proverbs 29:1

To be "broken beyond remedy" means to be past the point of no return. Sometimes a person's refusal to repent means the consequences of their sin will eventually destroy them completely. In the worst case, those who reject Jesus and refuse to repent of their sins must suffer the consequences of their sins forever. It breaks God's heart when this happens to people He loves and has forgiven at the cross. Some people just never repent.

So when you practice Relational Forgiveness, you must remember that you are giving people the **best opportunity to repent**. You cannot force them to repent. Even if you practice Relational Forgiveness perfectly as God does, some people will not respond favorably to painful but appropriate consequences. However, this brings us to one more key truth about repentance. Sometimes people repent not because of painful consequences, but something else altogether. Paul tells us what this is—

> *Or do you think lightly of the riches of His kindness and tolerance and patience, not knowing that the kindness of God leads you to repentance?*
>
> Romans 2:4

Sometimes kindness moves people to repentance.

We can see a picture of this in the movie "Les Misérables," which is all about a criminal released from prison. His name is Jean Valjean. He is homeless and is taken in for a night by a bishop and his wife. However, that night, fearful of his limited opportunities, he steals the family's silverware. The next day Jean is apprehended by the police, and is found in possession of a great deal of expensive silverware. They are sure he has stolen it. He tells them that the silverware had been given to him as a gift. Not believing him, the police bring him back to the bishop's home, ready to haul the thief back into prison as soon as the bishop confirms that the silverware was stolen. However, to everyone's amazement, the bishop affirms Jean's story, and asks Jean why he had not also taken the silver candlestick holders that he had given him. The police are shocked. The bishop's wife is shocked. The thief is shocked! The police leave and the wife goes to get the candlestick holders. The bishop and Jean are left alone in the garden.

Jean asks the bishop, "Why are you doing this?"

The bishop replies, "Jean Valjean, my brother, you no longer belong to evil. With this silver I bought your soul. I ransomed you from fear and hatred. Now I give you back to God."

The rest of the movie is about how this one act of extraordinary, unexpected and undeserved kindness changes Jean Valjean's life.

God's kindness can change people. When a person realizes just how kind, generous, merciful and gracious God has been toward him at such great cost to Himself at the cross, especially in view of his sinfulness and rebellion, he should become overwhelmed with thankfulness and love. This is a powerful truth. *Unexpected, undeserved and extraordinary kindness can motivate a person to repent.*

I say it "can" because, like painful consequences, kindness doesn't always work to bring about repentance. So which tool should we use: kindness or painful consequences? Both are appropriate. How do we know which one to use? We ask God to show us. Relational Forgiveness is flexible and dynamic. How it is done varies from situation to situation. We must pray and listen for God's directions on how and when to follow through with appropriate consequences for specific sins with specific people at specific times, and we must listen for God's direction on how and when to extend unexpected, undeserved and extraordinary kindness.

> "Unexpected, undeserved and extraordinary kindness can cause people to repent."

Fifth Principle. Establish God-authorized BOUNDARIES

Consequences and boundaries are very similar—in fact, boundaries are a kind of consequence. The difference lies in their purposes. The purpose of establishing God-authorized boundaries is to *protect future victims from an unrepentant person's future sins.*

Once, very late at night, Becky and I were driving home with the kids asleep in the car. We had to drive over a hill on a narrow, winding road with no shoulder. There was only one other car on the road, in front of us. As we started driving down the hill, the car in front of us started braking. It kept slowing down until it came to a stop in the middle of the road. I stopped behind him and waited. We waited a minute or two until we realized that something must be wrong. Carefully driving up beside him, I saw that the driver was unconscious at the steering wheel. I quickly drove up farther to a place where I could park and ran back to see what was wrong.

As I approached the car, I could hear music blasting out of the open window and smell the overwhelming smell of alcohol. I opened the driver's door and shook him. He woke up, but was clearly very drunk. Apparently he had passed out while driving down the hill, with his foot on the brake. I pushed him over to the passenger's seat, got into the car and drove to the nearest gas station. This was the first boundary I set up—I drove so he would not be able to. By the time we got there, he had passed out again. I parked his car, turned off the engine and put his keys in my pocket. This was the second boundary I set up—taking his keys meant that he would not be able to wake up and drive off while I called the police from the gas station (this was before cell phones).

> **The purpose of boundaries is to protect future victims from the sins of unrepentant people.**

When the police arrived, I assumed that my 'good citizen' duty was complete. I had protected others from a drunk driver. I had called the police. It was now three in the morning, and I needed to be at work by seven. I handed the keys to the officers and told them what happened. They believed me, but told me that they couldn't arrest the man. I was surprised. When I asked why not, they told me that they had not *seen him driving drunk*. Then they told me that *I could arrest him* (a citizen's arrest) because I had seen him driving drunk—but that if he pleads "not guilty," I would have to testify against him in court. They also cautioned me saying that if I went to court, he would see my face, have access to my name and address and could retaliate against me in the future.

I was frustrated! I was angry at this man who had jeopardized my life and my family's lives. He had interrupted our trip home, keeping me awake even later, and would mess up my next day. How far was this going to go? I didn't want any more of this. I wanted to go home, and I didn't want to put my family in danger by arresting him.

I returned to our car and told Becky the situation. We prayed and asked Jesus what He would do. Right then we remembered that God had punished Jesus for this man's sin of drunk driving. So we forgave him of the penalty for this sin. Then we decided that the most loving thing to do was arrest him, even if it put our family in danger, so he would feel the painful consequences of his sin and perhaps repent.

By arresting him, we were practicing not only the fourth but also the fifth principle of Relational Forgiveness. I was establishing another God-authorized boundary. If I had not arrested him, we and the police would have driven off, leaving his keys on the floor of his car. At some point he would have woken up, still under the influence of alcohol, and tried to drive home. In that condition he might have caused an accident and hurt or killed people. Arresting him prevented that from happening and also would result in a suspended license, hindering him from driving drunk again for some time. I was protecting future victims from an unrepentant person.

Like consequences, boundaries may be natural or administered by people. When they are necessary, we must be careful to use *God-authorized* boundaries. God could stop all sin by simply killing all people at any moment. However, that course of action does not meet God's greater desire, which is to **save as many people as possible from their sins**. When administering boundaries, we must be careful to keep God's ultimate goal in mind. For this reason, the fourth and fifth principles of Relational Forgiveness must be practiced in harmony and balance with each other, so that neither the victim nor the perpetrator are neglected or sacrificed indiscriminately—because God loves them both. (And we are all both victims and perpetrators of sin).

Sometimes victims are unable to set up appropriate boundaries for themselves. For example, wives are often unable to set up appropriate boundaries to protect themselves from an abusive husband—likewise for children of abusive parents. Many just don't have the strength, opportunity, courage or know-how to set up their own boundaries. In these cases, they need others to help them set up boundaries.

Practicing real forgiveness will lead to real love, and real love will always work to establish the best, God-authorized boundaries to protect victims of sin as much as possible, just as God does.

Sixth Principle. Evaluate the progress and ADJUST the consequences and boundaries as appropriate

Just as God forgives the consequences of our sins when we repent, we too need to be quick to change the negative consequences when we see people repent. Jesus himself said that withholding forgiveness from a repentant person is a sin in itself and has negative consequences.

> *For if you forgive others for their transgressions, your heavenly Father will also forgive you. But if you do not forgive others, then your Father will not forgive your transgressions.*
> Matthew 6:14-15

This sixth principle is about watching and determining whether the guilty person is becoming more or less repentant, then responding appropriately. If they are becoming more repentant, then the consequences need to be reduced and the boundaries lowered. However, if they are becoming less repentant and more hardhearted, then the consequences need to be increased and the boundaries heightened. This is why Jesus taught—

> *If your brother sins, go and show him his fault in private; if he listens to you, you have won your brother. But if he does not listen to you, take one or two more with you, so that by the mouth of two or three witnesses every fact may be confirmed. If he refuses to listen to them, tell it to the church; and if he refuses to listen even to the church, let him be to you as a Gentile and a tax collector.*
>
> Matthew 18:15-17

Loving relationships are damaged by sins. When one person doesn't want to repent, the relationship stays damaged and worsens over time. However, if a person becomes more repentant, sinning less and loving more, then a truly loving relationship can be established. This is the goal of Relational Forgiveness.

These are the six principles of Relational Forgiveness. Now let's look at how these principles work in each path of forgiveness.

The First Path of Forgiveness—Receiving God's Forgiveness of the Consequences of Our Sins Against Him

In this path, God is the one practicing Relational Forgiveness, and we are the ones responding to Him. He is giving us the best opportunity to repent of sins we have committed against Him. What does it look like to respond appropriately to God and repent?

- ### First Principle—Practice PERSONAL FORGIVENESS FIRST

  Jesus Christ has already paid the penalty for all of your sins—even the ones you don't know about and the ones you haven't yet committed. God has already forgiven you of the penalty and will not punish you for any of your sins. How are you responding to this good news? Are you eager to:

- *Identify your sins?*
- *Feel the reality of your sins together with God?*
- *Condemn your sins as God did?*
- *Embrace Jesus' execution as the full and just payment for your sins?*
- *Confess your sins to Him and thank Him for forgiving you?*
- *Rejoice in God's love for you?*

Repentance needs to begin with recognizing that God has already forgiven the penalty for that sin because of Jesus. Otherwise, you will be tempted to think that your repentance or deeds ('being good,' tithing, etc.) rather than the cross, is what causes God to forgive you of the penalty for your sin. As you repent of a sin, you need to continually remember, give thanks and embrace God's loving kindness towards you through Jesus Christ—it will help motivate your repentance.

- **Second Principle—Let the guilty person's level of REPENTANCE guide the process**

God wants to heal and restore you, but cannot do so until you repent. He desires that you see the futility and the hurtfulness of your sin, and turn away from it. He is working to motivate you to repent, and He lets your level of repentance guide what He does next.

- **Third Principle—Let REAL CHANGE verify authentic repentance**

God doesn't need to see our actions to know our hearts. He can see real repentance even before we act on it.

If God is not changing the consequences of your sin as much as you think He should, then perhaps you are not as repentant as you think you are.[26] How can we tell if our repentance is authentic? We need to look at our behavior. Are we just saying that we want to stop this sin in our lives, or are we doing something about it? Remember, truly repentant people will always try to do something different to let God change them.

---

26 Or perhaps it is a consequence that God cannot change at the present time for reasons we do not understand.

Why would a person not want to repent?

When a person believes that their sin is the **best possible way to meet their needs**, they will not want to give it up. Temptations always appeal to our needs—whether for love, significance, food, protection, companionship and even justice. God does want to meet all our needs, but in the best way—His way. We want to meet our needs in the quickest, easiest ways—which most often are sinful and harmful. However, sin never really fulfills our needs. It may seem to for some time, but ultimately it will only "steal, kill and destroy." When a sin just seems too attractive to reject, pray and ask God to show you what need this sin is appealing to. Ask God how He wants to meet that need in the best way, His way. Study and listen to His Word. Then follow His directions.

- **Fourth Principle—Follow through with appropriate CONSEQUENCES**

When we don't repent, there will be consequences; that's how God's world is ordered. God administers these consequences appropriately, without bias or discrimination. This isn't to punish us—Jesus has already taken care of our punishment. Rather, it is so that the negative consequences of sin motivate us towards repentance. If sins didn't hurt, people would not want to stop doing them. God allows and even administers these painful consequences in order to save us from our sin—just as a loving father would.

> *"My son, do not regard lightly the discipline of the Lord, nor faint when you are reproved by Him: for those whom the Lord loves He disciplines, and He scourges every son whom He receives." It is for discipline that you endure; God deals with you as with sons; for what son is there whom his father does not discipline? But if you are without discipline, of which all have become partakers, then you are illegitimate children and not sons. Furthermore, we had earthly fathers to discipline us, and we respected them; shall we not much rather be subject to the Father of spirits, and live? For they disciplined us for a short time as seemed best to them, but He disciplines us for our good, so that we may share His*

*holiness. All discipline for the moment seems not to be
joyful, but sorrowful; yet to those who have been trained by
it, afterwards it yields the peaceful fruit of righteousness.*

Hebrews 12:5-11

How do you respond to the negative consequences of your sins?[27] Do you complain? Do you get angry at God? Do you blame others? Do you disregard God's commands, thinking that it doesn't really matter how you live, and that you are free to do whatever you want without consequence? Do you use God's love and the cross as an excuse to continue sinning? Or do you take responsibility for your choices? Do you understand that when you put your hand on a hot stove you will get burned every time? Do you thank God for His commands and directions that are designed to protect you from sin? Do you thank God for His faithful love in constantly giving you the best opportunity to repent?

- **Fifth Principle—Establish God-authorized BOUNDARIES**

God uses many different kinds of boundaries to protect victims from unrepentant sinners. These boundaries may be natural or administered by someone's choice. They may be physical, emotional, economic, spiritual, relational, and legal or some combination of these. They may be temporary or permanent.

Physical death is one such boundary. Releasing people to hell, and then to an eternity in the Lake of Fire, is the ultimate, permanent boundary between those who reject Jesus and those who believe in Jesus. These two groups are living together now, but God will not allow this forever. People who reject Jesus and remain unrepentant will always destroy their world and people around them. God must separate them and establish an appropriate, permanent boundary between them.

---

27 Not all of the suffering in your life is a result of the consequences of your sins. Sometimes, it is because of the consequences of other people's sins. Be very careful not to blame yourself for other people's sins or to blame others for your sins

In this present world, however, God uses much less severe and temporary boundaries when appropriate and necessary—such as sickness, economic losses, jail, relationship breakdowns or weather, to name a few.

- **Sixth Principle—Evaluate the progress and ADJUST the consequences and boundaries as appropriate**

  God doesn't remove or decrease the negative consequences of a sin when we don't repent. However, as soon as we do repent, He is quick to change the negative consequences.

  If My people who are called by My name humble themselves and pray and seek My face and turn from their wicked ways, then I will hear from heaven, will forgive their sin and will heal their land.

  2 Chronicles 7:14

  As you repent, God can and will restore you to the life you were made for—the life that is in Him.

The Second Path of Forgiveness—Forgiving Other People of the Consequences of Their Sins Against Us

Someone has sinned against you. You are damaged. The relationship is damaged. You are angry. This person needs to stop doing this to you. This person needs to change, or else... You don't even want to love this person! What should you do? What does Relational Forgiveness look like?

1. Practice all three paths of PERSONAL FORGIVENESS FIRST

This isn't natural to us. We want to get even. We don't want to love our enemies! We have a hard enough time loving those who haven't hurt us, let alone those who have. However, if we continue in unforgiveness, we remain in brokenness, pain, limited freedom, unsatisfying relationships and disobedience to God. We need to be healed. This is why Personal Forgiveness must always come before Relational Forgiveness—otherwise, we will not have the right motives and the divine power to do what is right.

Unfortunately, we often skip this and go straight to trying to 'fix' the relationship—which usually means trying to 'fix' the other person. This makes us lose sight of what is happening inside of us.

> *Why do you look at the speck that is in your brother's eye,*
> *but do not notice the log that is in your own eye? Or how can*
> *you say to your brother, "Let me take the speck out of your*
> *eye," and behold, the log is in your own eye? You hypocrite,*
> *first take the log out of your own eye, and then you will see*
> *clearly to take the speck out of your brother's eye.*
>
> Matthew 7:3-5

When we try to correct someone else's sin without first correcting our own, Jesus says we are being a "hypocrite." Moreover, we will not be able to "see clearly to take the speck out of [our] brother's eye." This may come as a surprise, but God is more committed to changing the other person than you are. Your sin and brokenness, however, hinders you from joining Him in this. In fact, your sin may even be a bigger problem than their sin.

Hence, always pray and look for your own sins first. If God reveals any to you, make sure to confess them to God, believing that God has already forgiven you of the penalty because of Jesus, and repent. Next, ask God to show you how this person has sinned against you and not loved you the way He does. Make a list and work through the steps of Personal Forgiveness. If you have sinned against this person, confess it to them, asking them to forgive you because of what Jesus has done. As you do this, God will heal and free you. You will feel more of His love for this person and a greater desire to enjoy a loving relationship with them, if appropriate and possible. Only then are you really ready to start trying to give this person the best opportunity to repent.

2. Let the guilty person's level of REPENTANCE guide the process

At this point, let's assume we have practiced all three paths of Personal Forgiveness. We have received God's forgiveness and are at peace with God. We have forgiven this person and are not only free of our anger, but we truly want to be a part of God's blessing in this person's life. We have confessed our sins to them and have asked them to forgive us. Regardless of their answer, we are healed and have a clear conscience. What do we do next? First, we need to answer some questions, such as:

- *Do they know that they are sinning against us?*
- *Do they know how it is hurting us, them and the relationship?*
- *Do they care?*
- *Do they want to stop?*
- *Are they trying to stop?*

The answers to these questions will help you discover if this person is repentant at all, and if so, how much so.

Sometimes it is necessary to go further than just asking questions. Jesus said,

> *Be on your guard! If your brother sins, rebuke him...*
>
> Luke 17:3

Rebuking does not mean yelling, punishing or nagging. A biblical rebuke is a serious communication of truth, in love, with the goal of helping someone see their sin and encouraging them to stop. How they respond will tell you a lot about their level of repentance, which will help you to know what you need to do next.

3. Let REAL CHANGE verify authentic repentance

How can we know when someone is truly repentant?

Some people know how to say the 'right' things but have no intention of changing. Many others are self-deceived. They think they want to change, but in reality, deep down inside, they don't. Again, they will say the words of repentance, but they do not follow through with it.

Still others are captive to mental or physiological addictions or to demonic influences and are not as in control as they think they are.

Since we cannot see a person's heart, we must rely on outward behavior to verify authentic repentance. What does a person need to do to demonstrate real repentance? It depends on the person, their age, the sin, how often they have done it, how destructive it is, their relationship with us, etc. Again, the principle is simply this—Even if it doesn't work, truly repentant people will always try doing something different to change.

When someone says they are repentant and want to stop sinning against you in a particular way, say, "That's great! I'm so glad. What are you doing to let God change you so you will not do this again?" A truly repentant person will have a plan or be working on one—or may simply ask you for your help. An unrepentant person will either not understand the question or get defensive and angry.

As an example, let me finish the story about my son. When Michael dishonored me by misusing my guitar and rebelling against my directions to take care of it, I practiced Personal Forgiveness and let God heal me, freeing me of my anger. As I drove home, I wondered what I would find there. Would Michael still be playing his computer game? Would he be asleep, as it was now one in the morning? As his father, I was responsible for helping him mature into a responsible person. I knew that I needed to follow up on this sin and practice Relational Forgiveness, so I prepared myself for several different scenarios.

When I was about to open the front door, it opened on its own. Michael was on the other side, waiting for me. In my absence, Becky had helped him realize how much he had hurt me and why I was so angry. He felt God's conviction of his sin so deeply that it brought him to tears. He confessed his sin to God and received God's forgiveness. He also knew that he needed to ask me to forgive him, so he waited.

Before I could say anything, he hugged me. With eyes red from crying, he confessed his sin and asked me to forgive him. I was so thankful to God that I could say, "Of course I forgive you, Michael. I already did." This was Personal Forgiveness.

However, to know how I was to apply Relational Forgiveness, I still needed to know if he was really ready to change. I didn't yet know, so I said, "You know, you never had permission to use this guitar, and you didn't treat it very well when you did use it. As a consequence, you cannot use this guitar at all for two months and afterwards only when you ask me first. Is that okay with you?" (I administered a minor consequence because he already seemed motivated to repent). Michael said "yes" without complaint or hesitation. From this I could tell that Michael was likely to be sincerely repentant, because *truly repentant people are willing to suffer the consequences of their sin without complaint.* People who complain about and resist the consequences demonstrate that they don't really understand the severity of what they have done, how they have hurt those around them and their need to change. Now, Michael still needed to prove his repentance over time. If he'd started complaining about the consequences two weeks later or worse, if he'd even asked to use my guitar, I would have needed to talk with him more and increase the consequences. The happy ending to this story is that he not only accepted the consequence, but extended it voluntarily to demonstrate his repentance.

4. Follow through with appropriate CONSEQUENCES

All sins have consequences—most of which come naturally, without our intervention. Interrupting those consequences interferes with God's natural design in bringing people to repentance. Sometimes all we need to do is to get out of the way and let natural or automatic consequences run their course.

One summer, I took our three-year-old granddaughter out on a lake in a canoe. She had a life vest on so she would be safe even if she fell overboard. However, she needed to learn boat safety and follow her grandpa's directions. I told her to sit on the floor of the canoe and not stand up or lean over the side. Of course, like any child, she kept pushing the boundary, getting on her knees to reach out as far as she could, even though I kept insisting that she sit down. Finally, standing up a little, she reached out too far and fell into the water. Instantly, the vest had her upright. I grabbed her and lifted her back into the canoe. She was crying, cold and traumatized. I didn't need to administer painful consequences myself. Nature did that. I just held her and comforted her. When she calmed down, I explained why she had fallen out, why grandpa had told her to sit down and how her disobedience had landed her in the cold water. For months after that event, whenever she was tempted to disobey me, I would remind her of her plunge into the lake when she did not follow my directions. Just the reminder of it would always cause her to respond with careful obedience.

Sometimes, however, depending on the relationship we have with the person and the nature of the sin, we may need to administer consequences ourselves.

When I arrested the man who drove drunk, I was following through with an appropriate consequence — for him to spend a night in jail and be charged with his crime. It would have been appropriate (and loving) for me to testify against him in court. It would also have been appropriate for him to be found guilty and face the consequences decreed by the laws of our land.[28] Nature was not going to arrest him. I, and the legal system, had to do it.

It is very important to know that love is not a doormat. Love is neither codependent, nor an enabler. Love is strong. Sin doesn't have the position of power. Love does.

People who have become codependent to someone's sin often feel that they are doing what is loving—to just tolerate someone's sin, to let it slide or to absorb the cost and the pain. But letting someone sin and protecting them from the consequences is not love. God does not do that. Love knows that sin is destructive. Love wants to save people from sin, not allow them to continue in it. Love says, "I will do everything I can do to help you to stop sinning, even if it hurts me in the process."[29]

Love will suffer. Love will turn the other cheek. Love will go the extra

28 I never had to testify in court because he pled "guilty."

29 You might be wondering how this is not being codependent or an enabler. Codependency is a behavior that doesn't really try to stop someone from sinning. It only wishes the person would stop sinning, but is unwilling or unable to take the painful action necessary to give the offending person the kinds of consequences that might motivate him to change.

mile. Love will pay the price, but love is in charge when it chooses to pay the price. Love works hard to give a sinner the best opportunity to repent. Love follows through with appropriate consequences.

Now, the *appropriate* consequences for a particular sin vary greatly, depending on things like:

- *The age of the guilty person*
- *Your relationship with this person*
- *The kind of sin*
- *Whether it was committed deliberately, accidentally or in ignorance*
- *The number of times they have done it*
- *Whether they are still doing it*
- *The amount of damage it causes*

People respond to painful consequences differently. What motivates one person to repent may be considered trivial, therefore ineffective for someone else. As a general principle, apply the least painful consequences first and see if they work. If not, then introduce more painful consequences, and so on. Hopefully, these consequences will work before you exhaust all your options. If not, as Jesus said in Matthew 18:17, you must disconnect yourself from that unrepentant person, treating him as a Jew in Jesus' day would treat a tax collector or a Gentile and avoid close contact with them.

Remember, the purpose of all consequences is to help a person become more repentant—not to punish the guilty person or make you feel better. Punishment was dealt with at the cross. A person can also be brought to repentance by undeserved, unexpected and extraordinary kindness. You will need to pray and discern whether to use kindness or consequences—and if consequences, which ones.

5. Establish God-authorized BOUNDARIES

By arresting that drunk driver, I not only administered a consequence—I also established a God-authorized boundary. It prevented him from trying to drive when he regained consciousness, still drunk, and seriously hurting or killing someone, even himself. Arresting him protected those people. Moreover, the court would suspend his license, further hindering him from driving drunk again. So an action can actually be both a consequence and a boundary. In fact, all boundaries are a kind of consequence. It is their purpose that differentiates them—boundaries are for protecting others from an unrepentant person's sins.

Here are some examples of boundaries:

- *A restraining order*
- *Restricting access to money*
- *Not spending time with the person*
- *Supervised visitation*
- *Physical, residential or legal separation*
- *Reinforcing old rules or setting up new rules to be followed*

Like consequences, there are many possible God-authorized boundaries. Discerning which is appropriate in a given situation will depend on the same factors I listed under the fourth principle above.

We emphasize "God-authorized" because there are many effective boundaries that God would not approve for you to carry out. Shooting a perpetrator means he will never sin against you or others again, but we aren't to kill our enemies. We must not disobey God's commands or principles when we set up boundaries. Therefore, we must be careful to pray and study His Word in order to know the boundaries God would have us establish.

As with consequences, though there are exceptions, it is usually best to start with lower-level boundaries before working up to increasingly stringent ones if necessary. People can be so overwhelmed by excessive consequences and boundaries that they become despondent and give up. Wise counsel is often helpful in discerning and setting boundaries.

6. Evaluate the progress and ADJUST the consequences and boundaries as appropriate

As a person becomes more repentant and changes their behavior, we must be ready to reduce the consequences and boundaries. I say "reduce" because it is often inappropriate and even dangerous to simply remove all consequences and boundaries at once. Even a person growing in repentance may relapse into sin. They may make mistakes. We need to know how to encourage repentance without acting foolishly. Even a truly repentant person needs to rebuild the trust they lost—and that takes time.

Often, appropriate consequences and boundaries will motivate a person to repent. Real change will be demonstrated and we will be able to forgive the negative consequences of their sin. The relationship will be restored—or even better, it may grow stronger and healthier than before. Forgiveness doesn't just restore what used to be; real forgiveness creates something better. God is always building something better.

But this happy ending doesn't always happen. Some people just don't want to stop sinning, regardless of how painful the consequences might be or how much kindness they receive. After administering appropriate consequences and boundaries, one of two things will happen. The person will become either more repentant or less repentant.

An unrepentant person may become increasingly angry with those who are applying the painful consequences and boundaries. This is actually a good sign that the consequences are having a significant effect. Unfortunately, unrepentant people may resent us, cut us off, threaten us or try to hurt us. All this is to try and force us to stop putting pressure on them to stop sinning. In these cases, we need to keep practicing Personal Forgiveness as the person continues to sin against us. We will also want to persist and not surrender to their pressure to stop administering appropriate consequences and boundaries.

Practicing Relational Forgiveness effectively will move people in one direction or the other. I wish I could say that it always moves people to repentance and there always is a happy ending, but that's simply not true. Some people never repent and will suffer the consequences of their sins forever. Even so, administering the appropriate consequences and boundaries will minimize their destructive influence in our lives.

The Third Path of Forgiveness—Asking People to Forgive Us of the Consequences of Our Sins Against Them

In this path of forgiveness, the people we sinned against may not want to forgive us at all. They may be so hurt, so angry and so distrustful of us that forgiveness is inconceivable or even wrong. They may believe that it is impossible for us to change. But God is with us. He can change us, and over time we can demonstrate that change. When we do, it becomes increasingly difficult for people to withhold forgiveness. Hence, as important as they are, our words are not as important as our actions in this path of Relational Forgiveness.

God does not forgive the consequences of a sin when we ask Him, but when we repent. Similarly, people forgive us of the consequences of our sins against them not simply because we ask them to—no matter what words we use or how sincerely we ask—but because they see that we have truly repented. *When people can see that we are no longer the same person we were when we hurt them in the past, they may come to view and treat us differently.*

Having said that, however, if we don't confess our sins and ask them to forgive us, we will appear callous, hardhearted, indifferent and uncaring. They will not see repentance if we remain silent. We need to acknowledge our sin and responsibility for their pain and anger, and communicate to them our repentance as best we can.

> **The most important part of asking someone to forgive us of the consequences of our sins is the demonstration of our repentance.**

As in the first path of Relational Forgiveness with God, we are not really practicing the six principles as much as we are responding to the person we have sinned against. Whether or not they understand and are trying to practice real forgiveness, the truth of each principle still stands. You will have a much better opportunity to motivate someone to forgive you if you know these truths and cooperate with them, than if you ignore them.

What does it look like to ask someone to forgive you of the consequences of your sin against them?

1. *Practice all three paths of PERSONAL FORGIVENESS FIRST*

It is essential that we practice all three paths of Personal Forgiveness first. We need God to transform us to become more like Jesus if we are going to stop sinning against others the way we have been.

We also need to ensure we have forgiven the other person of the penalty for their sins against us. If not, our hurt and anger will sabotage our repentance, the sincerity of our request for them to forgive us and our motives for all these.

Finally, if we don't first help them to forgive us of the penalty for our sin against them, their hurt and anger will interfere with their motive and ability to forgive us of the consequences of our sin. For this reason, you may need to ask to be forgiven of both the penalty and the consequences of your sin at the same time, but for different reasons—the former, because Jesus suffered and died to pay for our sins, and the latter, because we are demonstrating sincere repentance.

2. *Let the guilty person's level of REPENTANCE guide the process*

When we see people broken and humbled by their past sins, when we see them trying hard to change, when they are changing, we naturally treat them differently from those who continue in their sins and do not change. In this path, you are the guilty person. The more people can see this change in you, the more likely they are to naturally change the negative consequences over which they have control. Most people will respond favorably to you according to your level of repentance.

170

3. Let REAL CHANGE verify authentic repentance

The key here is real, visible change. *What would the other person need to see from you that would convince them that you aren't the person you were when you sinned against them?* What do you need to do differently to demonstrate that God has changed you? If they see nothing different in you, don't expect them to treat you differently. Demonstrate change by treating not only them but all the people around you better than before.

4. Follow through with appropriate CONSEQUENCES

In this path of forgiveness we are the ones receiving the painful consequences. The question for us is this—*what is our attitude towards these consequences?* If we resist them, calling them unfair or getting angry at those who are administering them, then we will be demonstrating to all who are watching us that we aren't as repentant as we think we are. Truly repentant people feel the pain they have caused others and understand the severity of what they have done. Truly repentant people understand the reality that all sins have negative consequences, and are willing to accept that without complaint, anger or resistance. Truly repentant people surrender to these consequences, even when they are inappropriate.[30]

This doesn't mean that repentant people are powerless. On the contrary, they know that God will change them and their future for the best through their repentance. No matter how severe the earthly consequences may be, God can and will save a repentant person. He will heal, restore and give life to the fullest. A truly repentant person is willing to suffer humbly with their hope in God, not man.

---

30 When someone administers inappropriate consequences to you, they are sinning against you. It is very important that you forgive them of the penalty for this sin. Then you will need to ask God to show you how to humbly give them the best opportunity to repent and make the consequences of your sin more appropriate.

5. Establish God-authorized BOUNDARIES

Again, in this path, you aren't establishing boundaries—others are. So we are not really establing the boundaries; we are cooperating with them. Your response to boundaries will be very telling. If you resist them and do not cooperate willingly, then you will be demonstrating unrepentance. If you cooperate willingly and without complaint, then you will be demonstrating repentance.

6. Evaluate the progress and ADJUST the consequences and boundaries as appropriate

We cannot force people to forgive us of the consequences of our sins, but we can give them the best opportunity to do so by demonstrating repentance. We can pray and hope that they will see real change in us and choose to change the consequences. The more you repent and cooperate with God in changing you, the more reason people will have to forgive you of the consequences of your sin. However, even when they don't, God sees your repentance. He will reward you even if people don't. He will fulfill His promises to give you eternal life and goodness.

Forgiveness and Trust

The ultimate goal of forgiveness is to create loving relationships—and loving relationships involve trust. However, practicing forgiveness does not automatically guarantee a loving relationship or restore trust. Trust can be quickly lost because of a sin, and can take months or even years to regain. Sometimes it can never be regained.

Trust is the willingness to take a risk with someone who has the ability to hurt you. The more you trust someone, the more vulnerable you are to being hurt by them. Someone who sins against you demonstrates a real willingness to hurt you. If they do this repeatedly, or if their sin is severe, then they become more or even completely untrustworthy. So you cannot trust them as you did before, if at all.

Many people assume that forgiveness necessitates trust. However, you can forgive people and not trust them. Forgiving someone of the penalty for their sins against you allows God to change you, not the other person. If trust is to be rebuilt, they must change and prove that change over time. Likewise, you may practice all aspects of real forgiveness, but people do not have to trust you. You will have to work at earning back the trust you have lost.

Trust is difficult to rebuild, but it can be done. There are four basic principles for rebuilding trust. These will help us know how to rebuild the trust we have lost because of our own sins, and when to extend more trust to someone who has sinned against us.

- *Time*

  Change doesn't happen overnight. Real, significant change happens over time. It also takes time to prove that change is real and lasting. One good deed does not mean real change has taken place. Evil people can do all kinds of good things if it accomplishes what they want. Well-meaning people can do very good things for some time but then fall right back into their old patterns. We shouldn't trust those who have sinned against us just because they have done a few good things; nor should we expect the people we have sinned against to instantly trust us just because we did a few good things. Rebuilding trust takes time.

- *Transparency*

  Generally, unless we have reason to believe otherwise, we naturally extend some trust to one another. We don't assume the people we meet are murderers, rapists or thieves. So we also give a certain measure of privacy and freedom. However, when trust is broken by sin, and if we want to rebuild that trust, then that level of privacy and freedom must change. We must become transparent. That means voluntarily giving up some of our freedoms, allowing people to see us in ways they haven't before.

  For example, If you controlled the family checkbook, and broke trust by misspending the family's money, then becoming transparent might mean turning the control of the checkbook over to your spouse, or letting your spouse examine the checkbook at any time. If you have broken trust by visiting pornographic websites, transparency might mean using accountability software and allowing others to frequently check your web history at any time. If you have broken trust by lying about where you have been spending your time, then transparency might mean encouraging people to check in with you at any time, and you proving you are where you said you would be.

Transparency means allowing and even helping people see what we are doing when they want to see what we are doing. If we have really changed and are more trustworthy, then we will have nothing to hide from them. We will be willing and will even want to let them see what we are doing, because we are trying to demonstrate our new trustworthiness. If we hide anything, if we lie, if we are deceptive, then we will be found out and will lose more trust than ever before. It will be even harder and will take even longer for us to recover our trustworthiness.

- *Responsibility*

We give to the people in our lives a certain measure of trustworthiness which they maintain by living up to a **basic level of responsibility**, according to our expectations. However, when someone sins and demonstrates their inability to carry out this basic level of responsibility, they lose a measure of trustworthiness. Regaining their trustworthiness requires them to go beyond the first expected level of responsibility. They must demonstrate a higher level of responsibility—even more so if they want to recover their trustworthiness more quickly.

Think of it this way. Suppose you were in a car race. All the cars start at the same time. Everyone is driving at about the same speed, so no one is changing places. Suddenly your car has an unexpected problem. You pull into your pit stop and your crew is able to quickly fix it. You get back on the track. You are driving at the speed you were before, but now you are in last place. If you want to get back to the place you were before you stopped, you will need to drive faster than before, and faster than everyone else. Driving at the same speed you were before would just keep you in last place!

Similarly, in order to regain the trustworthiness we have lost, **we must become more responsible than we were before**. This means that we will need to try harder, pay more attention to details, let people see what we are doing, and avoid cutting corners. That's why we need Jesus living inside of us—only God can enable and empower us to be like Him.

- *Consistency*

If we want to rebuild trustworthiness, we must demonstrate consistency in our behavior. Consistency means doing the right thing each time in every situation.

If people know that we lie sometimes in some situations, they will know that we might lie in any situation, so we cannot be trusted to be honest all the time in every situation. If people know that we steal small things, they will know that we might also steal big things, so we cannot be trusted to guard their property in any and every situation. We need to be careful to be faithful in all things. As Jesus said,

He who is faithful in a very little thing is faithful also in much; and he who is unrighteous in a very little thing is unrighteous also in much.

Luke 16:10

Consistency is also best proven when there is a price to pay for doing the right thing. Anyone can tell the truth when there is nothing at risk. But if telling the truth means losing money, a job or popularity, then telling the truth becomes very difficult.

The golfer Bobby Jones exemplified the kind of character we need to have in order to rebuild trust. At the 1925 US Open, when he was about to take a shot, the head of his club brushed the grass and caused a slight movement of the ball. He took the shot, and then informed his playing partner Walter Hagen and the USGA official that he was calling a penalty on himself. Officials argued with Jones but he insisted that he had violated Rule 18—moving a ball at rest after address—and took a 77 instead of the 76 he otherwise would have scored. Jones's self-imposed one-stroke penalty eventually cost him the win by a stroke in regulation, necessitating a playoff, which he then lost. Although praised by many sports writers for his gesture, Jones reportedly said, "You might as well praise me for not robbing banks."

175

If the change in us is real, we will do what is right even when no one else is looking. To rebuild trust, we must be careful to demonstrate great responsibility and do it consistently. Otherwise, people will know that we're just faking it!

Final Thought

Only through repentance can God forgive and save us from the consequences of our sins and the sins of others. Every day, God is giving us the best opportunity to repent of our sins. If we really want to experience the fullness of God's life, we will repent of our sins as God reveals them to us, follow His pattern of Relational Forgiveness and do the same for others as well.

SUMMARY

- There are six principles to practice Relational Forgiveness well

    1. Practice all three paths of *Personal Forgiveness* first

    2. Let the guilty person's level of *repentance* guide the process

    3. Let *real change* verify authentic repentance

    4. Follow through with appropriate *consequences*

    5. Establish God-authorized *boundaries*

    6. Evaluate progress and *adjust* consequences and boundaries as appropriate

- The purpose of consequences is to motivate a person to repent

- The purpose of boundaries is to protect future victims from the future sins of an unrepentant person

- Sometimes undeserved, unexpected, extraordinary kindness leads to repentance

- We must ask God and seek wise counsel in choosing and establishing appropriate consequences and God-authorized boundaries

Trust can be rebuilt with:

    1. Time

    2. Transparency

    3. Responsibility

    4. Consistency

CHAPTER SEVEN

Developing a Lifestyle of Forgiveness

The Seventh Key Concept of Forgiveness

It is necessary to develop a lifestyle of God's forgiveness in order to fully experience Life

178

W hy is it so important to develop a lifestyle of authentic, biblical forgiveness?

Most people practice some form of forgiveness to solve an immediate problem, either in their emotions or relationships. However, to limit the practice of real forgiveness to just a few issues in your life would be like having a bank account with billions of dollars and only occasionally using it to go out for dinner. The value of practicing real forgiveness as a daily lifestyle is a wealth beyond comprehension. Here are some of its benefits:

- Peace with God
- Reduction/elimination of excessive painful emotions (i.e. anger, fear, depression, guilt, shame, etc.)
- Greater joy, peace, security and hope
- Elimination of self-condemnation
- Elimination of anger towards God
- A greater ability to feel God's love
- A greater ability to receive love from others
- A greater desire and ability to love others (even enemies)
- A greater ability to hear God clearly and receive truth
- Better decision-making
- Greater victory over persistent temptations
- Greater victory over compulsive behaviors
- Increased rest and relaxation
- The ability to set appropriate boundaries without feeling guilty
- Deliverance from demonic influences
- Better physical health (both natural and miraculous healing)
- A greater capacity for effective ministry
- Better opportunities to restore broken relationships
- Stronger marriages and families
- Less teenage rebellion
- More and better friendships
- Greater protection from hurtful and controlling people

In short, God wants you to experience all the fullness of His life in an overflowing abundance. Jesus said in John 10:10,

> *The thief comes only to steal and kill and destroy; I came that they may have life, and have it abundantly.*

Jesus made forgiveness possible, through which we can experience God's abundant life.

What Is Life?

Life—it is what God made you for, what your soul hungers for. You will never be satisfied with just existing, just surviving, just getting by. For all of humanity's desperate need for life, we have an amazingly poor understanding of what life really is.

Life is certainly more than just our biological machinery functioning well, or even continuing to function forever. There are many who are biologically alive but desperate to escape their seemingly hopeless existence.

Life is also more than material possessions. Having more stuff doesn't mean we will experience more life, though the world does everything to convince us otherwise. Very rich people are often very empty people.

Life is not in a place. It isn't found on a tropical island, or a beautiful city, or on a mountain top, or wherever you dream of. Being in a paradise doesn't make life happen.

Nor is life found in power, popularity, prestige, youth, music, accomplishments or anything else in this broken world. Life isn't found in anything the world has to offer.

Life is something completely different— that's why the world doesn't recognize or comprehend it. Yet we are all desperate for it. We cheat, kill and steal to try and obtain it, but always come up empty. So what is life?

> **Life is not found in anything the world has to offer.**

Life Is an Experience of Love

> *This is eternal life, that they may know You, the only true God, and Jesus Christ whom You have sent.*
>
> John 17:3

God is life.[31] To know God is to experience God's eternal life. God is also love.[32] The person who knows God also experiences love. Love and life are connected in God. In fact, the book of 1 John reiterates that God, Jesus, life, love, truth and light are so intricately connected that if a person has any one of these things, he has them all. Conversely, if a person does not have any one of these things, then he does not have any of them. Being connected to God makes us connected to life, love and truth.

To explain this further, when a person is connected to God through their faith in His truth expressed in Jesus Christ, he becomes able to *experience* God's life and love. Without God it is impossible to fully experience life and love.

I highlighted the word "experience" because life and love aren't just objects we possess. Life and love are dynamic expressions of who God is. God designed human beings to be able to experience Him and the life and love in Him. This is why God made us in His image.[33] We are not to just observe who God is—we are to experience Him personally and directly as He lives in us. Whenever we think, act or speak in real, God-like love, we are experiencing Him. We are experiencing life.

So I would like to suggest that life is an experience that happens when we are loving God and loving others as God does. When we are not doing this, we are sinning and experiencing death.

Love and Life Happen in Relationships

Love cannot happen in a relational vacuum—there must be at least two persons involved in giving and receiving love. We cannot experience love alone. Since love is life, this also means we cannot experience life alone!

This is why God said of Adam, before He created Eve, "It is not good for the man to be alone" *(Genesis 2:18)*. Adam was in a perfect, sinless, deathless world, and yet this was "not good." Adam was alone. He couldn't experience the fullness of life by himself. This is amazing because Adam had a loving relationship with God at this time! It means that God's design for humans to experience the fullness of God's life *must include love in*

---

31 John 1:1-4 and 14:6
32 1 John 4:8 and 16
33 Genesis 1:26-27

the context of human relationships. God has always been working to move people towards love. That's why Jesus said that *loving* God and *loving* others are the greatest commandments in the Law given to Israel.

> *"You shall love the Lord your God with all your heart, and with all your soul, and with all your mind.' This is the great and foremost commandment. The second is like it, 'You shall love your neighbor as yourself.' On these two commandments depend the whole Law and the Prophets."*
> Matthew 22:37-40

All of God's commandments are built on the foundation of loving God and loving others. Why does God so desire that we do this? It is because He wants us to experience the fullness of His life, because love is what life is all about and because love can only happen in relationships.

God Is Love—God Is Life

It is amazing that God is life all by Himself, since life is love, and love can happen only in relationships. But that's the very mystery of the Trinity. God is not alone when He is all by Himself. God is one Being but three distinct Persons — God the Father, God the Son and God the Holy Spirit. God is three loving relationships all by Himself—love between the Father and the Son, love between the Father and the Holy Spirit, and love between the Holy Spirit and the Son. God is love and God is life, all by Himself!

This is why John, the apostle, introduced Jesus this way,

> *In the beginning was the Word, and the Word was with God, and the Word was God. He was in the beginning with God. All things came into being through Him, and apart from Him nothing came into being that has come into being. In Him was life, and the life was the Light of men. The Light shines in the darkness, and the darkness did not comprehend it.*
> John 1:1-5

When Jesus became a man, it was as if God was turning on a light in an utterly dark world. The world was dark because it was saturated in sin and death. Jesus, being love and life, shone so brightly in the world that "the darkness did not comprehend it," or overcome it or control it. The world still doesn't comprehend Jesus or life because the world doesn't know what life really is. So people pursue the wrong things to try and meet their need for life.

Jesus invited people to Himself, saying,

> *I am the way, and the truth, and the life...*
>
> John 14:6

Jesus is *life*. He is the life we are looking for, the life the whole world is so desperately trying to find. He is the way through which we experience God's life. Why? Because Jesus is the way we can return to God and become loving persons.

Jesus Gives Life by Making It Possible for Us to Love

We don't naturally love God or each other the way God does. We love ourselves most. We are all sinful, broken people by nature—and we, by ourselves, cannot change our sinful nature! We need someone who can save us from who we are.

Jesus came to make it possible for us to experience all the fullness of God's life. How? He makes it possible for us to become people who love God with all our heart, soul, mind and strength, and who love our neighbor as we love ourselves. The more we love, the more we experience life.

The gospel of Jesus Christ is an invitation to return to God and let Him heal, restore, renew and transform us. This transformation begins when a person puts his trust in Jesus Christ as the only way he can be saved from the penalty, consequences and practice of sin. Upon that first act of faith, God the Holy Spirit comes into that person's soul and starts this

> "Jesus gives life by making it possible for us to love like God loves."

incredible work of transformation.

> *Therefore if anyone is in Christ, he is a new creature; the old*
> *things passed away; behold, new things have come.*
>   2 Corinthians 5:17

However, becoming a Christian is just the beginning of a lifelong journey. That's why Paul says,

> *...work out your salvation with fear and trembling; for it is*
> *God who is at work in you, both to will and to work for His*
> *good pleasure.*
>   Philippians 2:12-13

When God saves someone, He is saving them from something and into something. We are being saved from sin and into love, from death and into life. This is a lifelong process; we are to "work out" our salvation, we are to participate together with God.

In Romans 12:2, God directs us,

> *And do not be conformed to this world, but be transformed*
> *by the renewing of your mind, so that you may prove what*
> *the will of God is, that which is good and acceptable and*
> *perfect.*

In this verse we are told to be careful not to become like the world. Why? Because the world doesn't know what life is and where it comes from— God Himself. Instead, we are to "be transformed." This is an amazing word! It is the Greek word from which we get "metamorphosis."

Metamorphosis is the incredible process through which God completely recreates the entire organism—the skeletal system, nervous system, muscular system, digestive system... everything, without killing the animal in the process! I remember how difficult it was to convince my children that a caterpillar is a baby butterfly. Think about it. The caterpillar has huge chewing mandibles and eats leaves. Its body isn't much more than a worm. Yet a butterfly is known for its beautifully colored wings with which it can fly! Furthermore, butterflies don't have chewing mouthparts.

They have a roll-up straw through which they suck nectar from flowers.

Animals that undergo metamorphosis go through a transformation that is nothing short of a miracle! And this is how Paul describes the inner transformation that must happen in a person's life for us to become able to love like God loves. We don't need just a little tweaking, or a few good rules, or some better motivation, or an accountability group or a few Bible verses. Those are helpful, but what we really need is a complete reconstruction of our souls. If we are going to experience the fullness of life as God intended, then *we need to become people who are able to love God perfectly and love all other people just as God loves them*. In short, we need to become just like Jesus. And if you're like me, that's going to take a miracle!

God Transforms Us as We Practice Forgiveness

I believe there are six basic activities we need to practice to more rapidly and more deeply be transformed into the likeness of Jesus.

- Exposure to and assimilation of truth
- Practicing all aspects of real forgiveness
- Deliverance from demonic influences
- Personal experiences with God
- Making protective choices
- Creating nurturing environments

A Christian works out his salvation by practicing these six activities.

One of the most powerful, life-transforming activities—and unfortunately probably the least practiced in the church today—is practicing all aspects of real forgiveness. It is how God heals and thereby transforms the human soul. Thus, we need to learn how to develop *a lifestyle of authentic, biblical forgiveness* if we want to experience the fullness of life as God intended.

I find that most people do not have a lifestyle of forgiveness. Rather, they treat forgiveness like an emergency kit in the trunk of their car. If you have an emergency kit, let me ask—How often do you plan on using it? Of course, we would all say, "Never." We don't plan on being in an emergency, and we hope to never be in one. Emergency kits are *just in case* an emergency happens. People tend to think of forgiveness in exactly the same way—it's nice to have just in case you might need it someday.

However, in a world full of sin, where we sin and are sinned against every day, we need to be practicing forgiveness constantly. To do that, we need to do the work to develop a lifestyle of forgiveness.

When I was explaining this at one of our forgiveness seminars, a man said, "Oh, I get it. You want practicing forgiveness to be our second nature." I responded politely, "No, that's not quite correct. First of all, it's not what I, Steve Diehl, want for you. Practicing forgiveness is what God wants for you, and what you need. Second, God doesn't want practicing forgiveness to be your second nature, because that means something else is still your first nature. God wants practicing all aspects of His forgiveness *to be your first nature.*"

The more you practice forgiveness, the more God can transform you. It takes effort at first, but over time we can and should become as efficient at practicing forgiveness as we are at breathing.

Developing a Lifestyle Takes Work and Time

Developing any kind of lifestyle always takes work and time. A new lifestyle never happens automatically. I have heard it said that it takes at least 40 days of doing something new every day to make it a habit. And we are not talking about simply changing an eating habit or an exercise habit. We are talking about changing the way we think instinctively at the core of our being. Some of that may have already happened. I believe that having read this book, you are already starting to think differently about forgiveness.

However, it isn't just mentally knowing about a truth that transforms us. Rather, it is interacting with it.[34] You need to keep thinking about, praying about, meditating on, talking about and wrestling with God's truths about His forgiveness. You need to do things that will let God change the way you think about forgiveness.

Perhaps the most important principle about developing a new lifestyle is this—start practicing it right away. Don't wait until tomorrow, next week, when the house is clean or the bills are paid. Remember, practicing forgiveness is like riding a bicycle. No one learns to ride a bike in a classroom or by reading a

---

34 You might want to read this book again or use one of our other resources on biblical forgiveness at www.ForgivenessMinistries.org.

book. You have to get outside, get on a bike and try to ride it as best you can. You will fall down. You might even get a little injured. But if you keep it up, if you keep trying, you will eventually learn to ride a bike. And once you become good at it, you won't even think of what you are doing when you are riding, because it will have become first nature to you. So it is with developing a lifestyle of forgiveness. If you keep working on it, practicing it every chance you can, it will become your first nature.

So what sin can you confess to God *right now*, believing that Jesus has paid for it and that God has already forgiven you?

What sin can you repent of?

Who can you forgive of the penalty for their sin against you, knowing that Jesus died for them just as He died for you?

Has anyone truly and sincerely repented of their sins against you and you have not yet started to reduce the consequences and boundaries?

Who have you sinned against and have not yet, after receiving God's forgiveness and forgiving them, gone to them and asked them to forgive you? Are you ready to demonstrate your sincere repentance?

The best time to start is *right now*. Practice God's forgiveness. Let God heal you. Start a new lifestyle of authentic, biblical forgiveness.

Make a Plan to Go Farther

I'm so glad that you have read this book. In fact, I think that when you have finished it, you should celebrate. Enjoy an ice cream sundae, take a nap, walk in the park or anything you really enjoy. Just remember that if you put this book away and don't start doing some of the exercises, you will lose momentum, lose focus and forget what you started to learn.

You need to make a plan before it is too late. To help you, I've included below a list of things you can do to work towards developing a lifestyle of forgiveness. You don't need to do them all, and you can't do everything you may want to do all at once anyway. So make a plan, with deadlines and perhaps accountability. Most people need a partner, or two or three, to develop a new lifestyle habit. Who do you know that might want to develop a lifestyle of biblical forgiveness together with you?

These are just some of the things you can do to develop a lifestyle of forgiveness. You may think of some others. Again, be realistic. If your plan doesn't work for you then change it. Make it work. Just don't give up. Jesus came, suffered and died so that you could experience the fullness of His life. God has done His part. Now join with Him and do yours so He can heal you and set you free.

> *...work out your salvation with fear and trembling; for it is God who is at work in you, both to will and to work for His good pleasure.*
>
> Philippians 2:12-13

God's good pleasure is to heal and transform you into a truly loving person. And the more you love, the more you will experience life in all its fullness as God intended for you experience it.

DEVELOPING A LIFESTYLE OF FORGIVENESS ACTIVITY

CHOOSE JUST A COUPLE OF THESE WITH WHICH TO BEGIN, AND THEN ADD TO THEM AS YOU HAVE SUCCESS.

I WILL DO THIS *(MARK ACCORDINGLY)*   WHEN?

☐ I will pray and ask God to help me to develop a lifestyle of biblical forgiveness. *NOW*

☐ I will use the "Identifying My Substitutes for Forgiveness" worksheet at the back of the book to discover my coping mechanisms and ask God to help me to see when I am doing them. _____

☐ I will memorize the definitions for Personal Forgiveness and Relational Forgiveness. _____

☐ I will memorize the six basic steps of Personal Forgiveness. _____

☐ I will memorize the six principles of Relational Forgiveness. _____

☐ I will tell two or three people close to me that I am committing myself to God to develop a lifestyle of forgiveness, and ask them to point out to me when I am not practicing forgiveness but rather am using one of my coping mechanisms, or otherwise demonstrating symptoms of inner brokenness. _____

☐ I will find two or three people who also want to develop a lifestyle of forgiveness and we will help each other to do this. _____

☐ I will start a forgiveness small group. ———

☐ I will ask God regularly to show me my sins and the sins others have committed against me. ———

☐ I will set aside time to confess one sin each day. ———

☐ I will set aside time to forgive one person each day. ———

☐ I will read though this book again. ———

☐ I will find two or three 'safe' people who will empathize with my pain and anger and share my story with them so I can better feel God's comfort and validation. ———

☐ I will help a hurting friend practice forgiveness. ———

☐ I will give this book as gift to two or three people.
They are:
-
-
-
- ———

☐ I will become a friend of "Focus on Forgiveness" on Facebook. ———

☐ I will use my stories of forgiveness to help motivate others to practice forgiveness. ———

☐ I will help my Sunday School class or cell group focus on forgiveness. ———

☐ I will start a forgiveness ministry emphasis in my church. ———

SUMMARY

- God made human beings to need to experience life
- God is life
- God is love
- Life and love are connected
- Life is an experience that happens when real love happens
- We experience life when we love God and when we love others the way God does
- We need to be transformed by God into the likeness of Jesus in order to be able to love
- The more we love, the more we experience life
- Practicing biblical forgiveness is one of the most powerful ways God transforms us
- We need to develop a lifestyle of forgiveness if we want to experience the fullness of love and life as God intended

CONCLUSION

In *John 4:7-26*, John records an encounter that Jesus had with a woman in Samaria. As a Samaritan, she was scorned by the Jews. As a woman, she was abused by the chauvinistic attitudes and practices of her culture. Having been married five times and now living with another man, she was a social outcast. Because she was rejected by her community, she came alone in the heat of the day[35] to draw water. Jesus was sitting by that well.

So he started a conversation with her by saying, "Give me a drink."

She was shocked! How could he, a Jew, a man, a rabbi, even speak to her? She objected, saying, "How is it that you, being a Jew, ask me for a drink, since I am a Samaritan woman?"

Jesus responded, *"If you knew the gift of God,* and who it is who says to you, 'Give me a drink,' you would have asked him, and he would have given you living water."

Confused, she asked Jesus where this "living water" was and how it compared to the water in the well.

Jesus said, "Everyone who drinks of this water *will* thirst again; but whoever drinks of the water that I will give him shall never thirst; but the water that I will give him will become in him a well of water springing up to eternal life."

---

35 Women normally came to draw water in the morning, in the cool of the day, and did so together with other women for friendship and conversation.

She was created for Life. She needed and wanted Life, but she was experiencing death. She was dying of thirst for living water. *Jesus is the living water*. He is the gift of God who quenches our thirst for real Life because He makes forgiveness possible, through which we are able to experience Life.

Like that woman, God created you for the fullness of His life. And like that woman, He knows that you aren't yet fully experiencing His Life. He knows that you are thirsty. He wants to quench your thirst. He wants to heal you of the damage you have sustained from so many sins. He wants to set you free and fill you with life, love and joy. He wants you to receive His gift of Life in His Son Jesus Christ through your practice of *all aspects* of His forgiveness.

As you learn to practice His forgiveness, you will be drinking from God's well of Life. Drink deeply. Drink often. You will be satisfied.

Now may our God and Father, and our Lord Jesus Christ, bless you richly as you learn to practice all aspects of His forgiveness. Amen.

IDENTIFYING
MY PERSONAL
SUBSTITUTES FOR
FORGIVENESS

Practicing authentic forgiveness does not come naturally. However, practicing a substitute for forgiveness does. The most typical substitutes for forgiveness are briefly described below. You have done all of them at one time or another, but you specialize in just a few. They have become so natural to you that you are probably unaware that you are even doing them! They have become a part of your personality. After reviewing the descriptions of the substitutes, follow the directions for the worksheets. This exercise will help you to discover your primary personal substitute for practicing authentic forgiveness.

Sins travel in three directions—we sin against God, other people sin against us and we sin against other people. People use the following substitutes to cope with the pain and debilitating effects of sins.

Manage our emotions— When we are feeling an emotion we do not like to feel, we tend to block it out or replace it. We reject uncomfortable emotions and try to feel comfortable ones. This can be done through denial, a change in activity, or drugs.

Exercise self-control— When we think about doing something inappropriate, we tend to restrain ourselves so as to not act out what we are thinking or feeling. Self-control is a good thing, but it is not forgiveness.

Overlook sins— We are so used to seeing sin in everybody, we tend to overlook sins, especially those we would call "little sins." Most sins just don't catch our attention.

Misidentify sins— Culture, family and personal rebellion against God make it difficult for us to correctly identify sins. We can call something a sin when it is not. And we can believe something is not a sin when it is. God defines sin, not people.

Blame the wrong person for sins— We tend to blame ourselves for other people's sins and we tend to blame other people for our sins. We can even blame God for our sins!

Try to forget about sins— If something makes us uncomfortable, we tend to avoid it by not thinking about it. This can be done consciously and subconsciously (selective amnesia).

Minimize sins— We tend to compare one sin with other sins and "grade it on the curve." Lesser sins are minimized when we start thinking "Well, it is not as bad as ..."

Excuse sins— We tend to find reasons why certain sins were unavoidable.

Justify sins— We tend to find reasons why certain sins were not only unavoidable, but appropriate and necessary!

Deny sins— We tend to deceive ourselves into believing that the sin did not happen, or at least was not a real sin.

Ignore sins— We tend to think that "time heals all wounds" and that if we just ignore the sin, it and its consequences will just go away.

Hide from sins— We tend to run away, physically or mentally, from sin, to escape having to face it head on. We can use all kinds of good and bad things to hide from sin, such as work, pleasure, drugs, alcohol, activity, inactivity, etc. to avoid dealing with it.

Tolerate sins— We tend to accept sins as normal and inescapable, so we tolerate most of them.

Punish someone for sins— We tend to try to punish the guilty person or someone else, even the victim of the sin.

Compensate for sins— We tend to "make up" for sins by doing good things. We also tend to modify our behavior in unhealthy ways to keep other people from sinning against us again.

"Let it go."— We tend to try to "move on" and not let the sin affect us any more. Many psychological tools can be employed to do this. However, it is usually a combination of several of the other substitutes for authentic forgiveness.

We all have done all of these. They come very naturally to us. However, each person learns from childhood to specialize in just a few of them. Which ones do you specialize in?

There are three worksheets which follow, one for each path of sin. All sixteen substitutes for forgiveness are listed on each worksheet. Put a letter "A" next to the substitutes you do most frequently. Then look for the one you least frequently do and put the letter "C" by it. Put a letter "B" by the rest. Do not worry too much about the middle group. The goal here is to see what you do most frequently and what you do least frequently.

Then follow the directions on the remaining worksheet at the end of this exercise.

Knowing which substitutes you do automatically will help you to resist them and to replace them with authentic forgiveness. In addition to your own answers, you may want to ask someone who knows you very well (your spouse, your mom or dad, or a close friend) to fill out the first three worksheets. Their perspective may help you to see yourself more clearly.

Ask God to help you to identify your substitutes for forgiveness so that you can replace them with real forgiveness.

HOW DO I USUALLY DEAL WITH MY OWN SINS *AGAINST GOD?*

____ Manage my emotions—I try to force myself to feel something different than what I am feeling.

____ Exercise self-control—I discipline myself not to act out what I am thinking or feeling.

____ Overlook my sin—I don't let it catch my attention.

____ Misidentify my sin—I think something is not a sin when God says it is and/or think something is a sin when God says it is not.

____ Blame the wrong person for my sin—I blame someone else for my choices and actions.

____ Try to forget about my sin—I refuse to let my mind dwell on it.

____ Minimize my sin—comparing my sin to "worse" sins and thereby lessen my sense of need to deal with it. "It's not as bad as ..."

____ Excuse my sin—"Everyone else does it!"

____ Justify my sin— I believe I had valid reasons for doing this.

____ Deny my sin—I do not believe I am guilty of the accusation. "I didn't do it!"

____ Ignore my sin—I think that my sin and its consequences will go away with time if I just ignore it.

____ Hide from my sin—I run away, physically or mentally, from my sin, perhaps using work, pleasure, drugs, alcohol, activity, inactivity, etc. to avoid dealing with it.

____ Tolerate my sin—I accept it as normal and decide not to do anything about it.

____ Punish someone for my sin—I punish either myself, other people or God for my sin.

____ Compensate for my sin—I try hard to be better or pay for my sin.

____ "Let it go."—I try to "move on" and not let my sin affect me any more.

HOW DO I USUALLY DEAL WITH THE SINS OF OTHERS *AGAINST ME?*

___ **Manage my emotions**— I try to force myself to feel something different than what I am feeling.

___ **Exercise self-control**— I discipline myself not to act out what I am thinking or feeling.

___ **Overlook their sin**— I don't let it catch my attention.

___ **Misidentify their sin**— I think something is not a sin when God says it is and/or think something is a sin when God says it is not.

___ **Blame the wrong person for another person's sin**— I blame myself or someone else for a particular person's choices and actions.

___ **Try to forget about their sin**— I refuse to let my mind dwell on it.

___ **Minimize their sin**— comparing their sin to "worse" sins and thereby lessen my sense of need to deal with it. "It's not as bad as ..."

___ **Excuse their sin**— "Everyone does it!"

___ **Justify their sin**— I believe they had valid reasons for doing what they did.

___ **Deny their sin**— I do not believe they are guilty of the accusation. "They didn't do it!"

___ **Ignore their sin**— I think that their sin and its consequences will go away with time if I just ignore it.

___ **Hide from their sin**— I run away, physically or mentally, from their sin, perhaps using work, pleasure, drugs, alcohol, activity, inactivity, etc. to avoid dealing with it.

___ **Tolerate their sin**— I accept it as normal and decide not to do anything about it.

___ **Punish someone for their sin**— I punish either the guilty person, myself, other people or God for someone's sin.

___ **Compensate for their sin**— I try hard to be better or to pay for their sin.

___ **"Let it go."**— I try to "move on" and not let their sin affect me any more.

HOW DO I USUALLY DEAL WITH MY SINS *AGAINST OTHERS?*

___ **Manage my emotions—** I try to force myself to feel something different than what I am feeling.

___ **Exercise self-control—** I discipline myself not to act out what I am thinking or feeling.

___ **Overlook my sin—** I don't let it catch my attention.

___ **Misidentify my sin—** I think something is not a sin when God says it is and/or think something is a sin when God says it is not.

___ **Blame the wrong person for my sin—** I blame someone else for my choices and actions.

___ **Try to forget about my sin—** I refuse to let my mind dwell on it.

___ **Minimize my sin—** comparing my sin to "worse" sins and thereby lessen my sense of need to deal with it. "It's not as bad as ..."

___ **Excuse my sin—** "Everyone else does it!"

___ **Justify my sin—** I believe I had valid reasons for doing this.

___ **Deny my sin—** I do not believe I am guilty of the accusation. "I didn't do it!"

___ **Ignore my sin—** I think that my sin and its consequences will go away with time if I just ignore it.

___ **Hide from my sin—** I run away, physically or mentally, from my sin, perhaps using work, pleasure, drugs, alcohol, activity, inactivity, etc. to avoid dealing with it.

___ **Tolerate my sin—** I accept it as normal and decide not to do anything about it.

___ **Punish someone for my sin—** I punish either myself, other people or God for my sin.

___ Compensate for my sin—I try hard to be better or pay for my sin.

___ "Let it go."—I try to "move on" and not let my sin affect me any more.

LIST THE SUBSTITUTES FOR FORGIVENESS YOU USE MOST FREQUENTLY FOR EACH OF THE THREE PATHS OF SIN.

The main ways I cope with my sins *against God*.

_____

_____

_____

_____

_____

_____

The main ways I tend to cope with other people's sins *against me*.

_____

_____

_____

_____

_____

The main ways I tend to cope with my sins *against other people*.

_____

_____

_____

_____

_____

Is there a pattern?

_____

If so, what is it?

_____

Why do you think you choose to deal with sin in this way?

_____

_____

_____

_____

_____

_____

A prayer to pray:

> *"Father, I acknowledge to you that I have developed a pattern of dealing with the sins in my life in ineffective and ungodly ways. I do not want to do so any longer. I want to deal with sin in the right way, the way you deal with it through Jesus Christ. Thank you for forgiving me. Please show me how to practice all three paths of forgiveness so You can heal me and set me free. Amen."*

204

29211829R00117

Made in the USA
San Bernardino, CA
12 March 2019